DUTCH POTTERY AND PORCELAIN

NEWNES' LIBRARY OF

THE APPLIED ARTS

JAR WITH COVER, enamelled earthenware of Delft; octagonal and fluted, painted in polychrome, marked by Louwys Fictoor at the sign of "The Double Bottle." Late XVII century. Height 30 inches.

DUTCH POTTERY *and* PORCELAIN

BY

W. PITCAIRN KNOWLES

LONDON
GEORGE NEWNES LIMITED
Southampton Street, Strand; W. C.
NEW YORK
CHARLES SCRIBNER'S SONS

CONTENTS

LIST OF ILLUSTRATIONS

LIST OF ILLUSTRATIONS

PREFACE

HEN it was first suggested to me that I should write a book on Dutch Pottery and Porcelain, my thoughts turned at once to the country in which I had lived for so many years. It was gratifying to me to have an opportunity of, figuratively speaking, going over the ground again, and to recall the names of towns and streets, the small dealers in out-of-the-way corners, and the more important ones at whose establishments fine specimens could always be procured, provided that one had no objection to paying fine prices for them.

My own collection came into being very gradually; a piece here, a specimen there—sometimes acquired for its curiosity, sometimes for the quaintness of its decoration, its fine colour, or the beauty of its glaze. In those days Delft pottery was not so much sought after as it was later; now the prices of the finer examples are almost prohibitive. The history of the potteries had not then been written so fully; and the names of the potters and of their factories had not been arranged and classified methodically; and consequently it was difficult to attribute a piece, by means of its mark, to its rightful maker. But being regarded in Holland almost as a native, I was able to pick up much useful information from the dealers, many of whom seemed to look upon me as a promising pupil. The information gleaned was of a thoroughly practical nature, and therefore of considerable value, but the names of the makers and the manner in which they worked and the locality of their potteries still remained a mystery as regards many of the marks.

With the appearance of M. Henri Havard's book on Delft pottery the curtain was lifted, and each potter and every pottery now has its place assigned in the history of the craft. The publication of this work had a twofold effect. It was of great assistance to the collector, but it also opened the eyes of the dealer to the value and importance of the examples in his possession. The number of collectors increased, and prices rose in unison. But this made the hunting more exciting, and led one into strange places—into the byways off the beaten track. The hunter's instinct received a fillip from the necessity of groping into likely nooks and corners, and tracking the quarry to its lair with nothing but hearsay and report as a guide.

But my commission covered a wider field; it extended to the porcelain as well as to the potteryware of Holland; and the chief difficulty to overcome was the proportionate assigning of each branch to its proper place, for Delft overshadows all the other factories. It is a giant of world-wide fame amongst pigmies of whom little is known.

In arranging this volume I have endeavoured to keep always in view the difficulties I myself had to contend with as a collector, and I have attempted to supply such information as regards the history of Dutch porcelain and pottery, and the quality and character of the produce, as may be a guide to the collector and student in attributing specimens to the correct maker and factory and period. I have, in fact, made an effort to supply what I felt the need of, but could not obtain, when I began collecting.

I need not, perhaps, tell the reader that he will have to buy his experience with the mistakes he makes. There is an enormous quantity of imitation Delft in circulation, but if the collector should come into possession of a specimen of the spurious article, and will compare it with a genuine piece, he will find it of considerable assistance as a guide to help him to avoid mistakes in the future.

Holland is a rather expensive hunting-ground for all kinds of curios, but even in the smallest towns the collector will find dealers from whom he can obtain not uninteresting specimens of Delft, and at the larger establishments at the Hague and Amsterdam he will, at any rate, be gratified with the variety and quality of the charming examples displayed, even if he is stunned by the uniform altitude of the prices asked for them.

Some years having elapsed since the dispersal of my own collection and the final cessation of my quest, I found it necessary to refresh my memory on several points by reading again the works on the subject of Delft pottery by Mr. Demmin, M. Jacquemart, and M. Henri Havard; and these books have afforded me the same pleasure and interest and admiration as when I first consulted them thirty years ago. I am also indebted to the authorities of the Victoria and Albert Museum, South Kensington, and of the British Museum, for their courtesy and kindness in allowing me special facilities for closely examining many interesting specimens under their care, and for enabling photographs to be taken wherewith to illustrate this book.

W. P. K.

USEFUL BOOKS OF REFERENCE

"**Histoire de la Céramique.**" Par JACQUEMART.

"**Histoire de la Faience de Delft.**" Par HENRI HAVARD.

DELFT DISH, in enamel of the characteristic greenish tint, painted in oriental style in variously-coloured enamels. Marked on the back in red in imitation of Chinese or Japanese marks. Probably an early specimen. 13 inches by 11 inches. South Kensington Museum.

DUTCH POTTERY AND PORCELAIN

CHAPTER I

POTTERY AND PORCELAIN

ORCELAIN, or, as it is called in English, China, was already known in Europe in the sixteenth century. The Portuguese navigators had brought some specimens from the East, but it was only after 1602 that the Dutch East India Company was the means of making this new discovery more generally known.

It would be interesting to find out in what form and shape these first importations of porcelain appeared, for thereby we might be able to obtain some idea of the impression or influence they had on public opinion at that time. We have ample evidence to show that the decorative qualities of these new arrivals contributed in a marked way to stimulate the artistic branch of the potters' trade, notably at Delft.

The principal reason, however, why this new product created such a name for itself all over Europe must have been the quality of the material of which it consisted. The pottery in use was of a coarse clay, brown in colour, heavy, thick, and liable to fracture; whereas the new importation was perfectly white, and even translucent, and it possessed qualities that enabled it to be moulded and shaped into vessels of a strength and lightness unattainable in the case of pottery. It is not surprising, then, that the potters of all nations tried to imitate it.

If we are to believe the Italians, they were the first to make the attempt; the French followed, and then the Germans. But failure succeeded upon failure until a clue was found by one Bötger, at Meissen, near Dresden, in 1717.

It was fortunate for these first explorers into the Chinese secret that they were encouraged, protected, and supported financially by illustrious persons. It is evidence of the captivating powers of this new craze, and of the value at which it was esteemed, that Royalty should have been its champion. To place sentries over the workman's house for fear the secret might leak out, to bribe a foreman to another Court where honours and protection awaited him, was the serious business of King, Prince, and Potentate.

And so it came about that throughout

DELFT PLAQUE, painted in blue, with landscape by H. Mommers. Date about 1660. Height 14 inches. Franks collection, British Museum.

Germany from Berlin to Vienna, all over France, from Genoa to Naples, from Copenhagen to Petersburg, the wandering German found his way to Holland.

There are, however, two kinds of porcelain—the soft or tender paste, and the hard paste. Both are in appearance the same, but the touch or feel and the weight betray the difference. It is the material used for the making that distinguishes the one from the other. Soft-paste china is in reality a kind of faïence or better sort of earthenware, but translucent clear, though not transparent. Hard-paste porcelain is of considerably later date, for its essential matter was only discovered in the beginning of the eighteenth century. This is the koalin, a Chinese name for the clay used. It is found in China, Japan, Saxony, Cornwall, and Limoges, the clay of China, Japan, and Cornwall being peculiarly white.

It is not surprising that, after the attempts to manufacture soft-paste china had proved that the quality and hardness of the Oriental ware could not be achieved, the use of China clay in those European countries that possessed it should have started simultaneously, or nearly so—namely, during the first half of the eighteenth century.

The manufacture of soft-paste china preceding the hard-paste, was a step from earthenware to porcelain, both in the matter employed and in the process of making.

It will be stated in another chapter of this work how some of the Delft potters reached an amount of skill in their craft that enabled them to produce plates, cups, and saucers of a thinness and lightness that equalled the Chinese importations; in fact, some of these specimens were considerably lighter, for china is heavier than Delft ware or soft-paste porcelain. There were potters at Delft who claimed that they had discovered the secret of making porcelain such as the Chinese made, and the name of this ware—china—is given to distinguish it from the earthenware then made in Holland. But this subject must be postponed to a future chapter, although it may be recorded here that soft-paste porcelain was made in Holland at this period, even if we cannot attribute it to any special place or maker.

If, however, there was an advance in the quality of the manufactured article, from earthenware to soft-paste porcelain, and then to the hard-paste, the colouring in the way of decoration suffered. No painting on hard-paste china can ever approach the brilliancy

DELFT SCONCE of earthenware, painted in blue, with raised scroll borders and a shield of arms in the centre surmounted by a crest. XVII century. $15\frac{3}{4}$ inches by 11 inches. Bandinel collection, South Kensington Museum.

DELFT PLATE of enamelled earthenware, painted in blue. One of a set of twelve, representing the different phases of the tobacco trade in the XVII century. Diameter $10\frac{1}{2}$ inches. Second half of XVII century. Collection of J. H. Fitzhenry, Esq.

of that on Delft earthenware, nor does it equal the effect produced on soft-paste porcelain.

The reason is due to the process of manufacture. In Delft ware, as in soft-paste china, the colouring is painted on the unbaked clay. When placed in the oven a temperature is reached sufficient to bake the clay, but the heat is not so excessive as to injure the colours, and they amalgamate and are fused with the glaze. This mixture of glaze and colour gives the extraordinary brilliancy to the colouring of Delft ware that places it beyond the rivalry of any other kind of earthenware, porcelain, or china in Europe. It is Delft's chief characteristic.

Soft-paste porcelain is the nearest approach to it, and that is why the collector will give such high prices for the finer specimens in this quality; at least, that should be the reason of its being so sought after, but it may be that some buyers simply acquire such examples because they imagine, in their innocence, that the rarity consists in its being soft-paste, and not hard-paste.

Soft-paste porcelain was not allowed to rest on the floor of the oven during the process of baking; it was suspended on wires, or it was placed on tripod stands, and the foot or base not being in contact with anything, the glaze covered the bottom of the base entirely. Hard-paste was placed on the floor of the oven, and the base, or such part which stood against the floor, remained without a glaze covering, leaving the rough surface of the clay exposed.

Hard-paste is heated to a white heat at a temperature that would completely destroy all colouring; it is decorated or painted afterwards, and rebaked sufficiently to attach the colour to the glaze, but it is never fused or absorbed in the enamel as in the case of Delft, and also of the soft-paste porcelain. The glaze of Delft and soft-paste is thin and friable, like a coating of varnish. The glaze may be scratched through with a sharp instrument quite easily, and the exposed clay will yield to the point. On the other hand, the glaze of hard-paste will resist any ordinary efforts to penetrate the surface, as will also the underlying clay, which has the character of glass; but the colouring on hard-paste will suffer by contact with rough surfaces, because it is not fused in the glaze, nor has it the enamel to protect it.

When broken, hard- and soft-paste show no difference of material; they are both white.

DELFT PLAQUE, painted in blue, with landscape after Berghem. About 1660. Height 14 inches.

Hard-paste has this advantage over its two other rivals, that it is much stronger and it will stand a much greater amount of heat, not being liable to fracture under the influence of violent changes of temperature. The two pastes may be distinguished the one from the other by the sense of touch, but this is a faculty to be acquired; a sense of touch cannot be explained or taught. Mr. Gladstone, who was a collector of porcelain, is supposed to have said that Chelsea "had the feeling of firm baby's flesh."

CHAPTER II

PORCELAIN

THE porcelain factories of Holland do not seem to have flourished. Without Royal encouragement, they depended on private means of support. A pastor, a certain Dr. Moll, appears to have devoted considerable efforts to establishing and reviving an industry that seemed incapable of overcoming the preliminary difficulties that often attend new undertakings. The lives of these factories are so short that there is little to chronicle as regards their existence; and what we learn is generally cut short by financial troubles or the removal of men and plant to some other locality.

In 1614, one Wytmans, at the Hague, took out patent rights for the period of five years for making, throughout Holland, all kinds of porcelain, similar in material and

DELFT PLATE, with landscape. Date about 1660. Diameter $8\frac{2}{5}$ inches. British Museum.

DELFT PLATE of enamelled earthenware, painted in blue. One of a set of twelve, representing the different phases of the tobacco trade in the XVII century. Diameter 10½ inches. Second half of XVII century. Collection of J. H. Fitzhenry, Esq.

decoration to that made in foreign countries—the foreign countries being, of course, China and Japan, whose importations were so much sought after in the seventeenth century. We shall see, however, that some of the potters at Delft boasted that they could make their ware as the Chinese did, and they announced it as such and advertised it. They even called their factories *Porselein Fabrieken*, as distinguishable from *Plateel Bakkerÿ*, which was the common name for the earthen-ware factory; but though they called this ware porcelain, it was probably no more than a great improvement, owing to its thinness, lightness, and better decoration, on what had been usually produced. But we should also consider this important fact, that the authorities at the Hague would not probably have granted such important rights and privileges to Wytmans to make this supposed new china unless it were really such; for if it were only pottery-ware, the patent would infringe the rights of the Guild of St. Luke and the Delft potters. It may, therefore, be porcelain that was really meant. Some one has, however, stated that there is a specimen of this product in existence marked with a "W" and the word "'sHaag," which, as well as the word "'sGravenhage," is the Dutch for the Hague—it means the Count's fence or hedge.

This assertion shrouds the matter in greater mystery than ever, when we might expect it to be a clue to an escape from the dilemma of uncertainty. It might be a valuable discovery if we could see this specimen—for form, design, colour, and material, no less than an indication of the period by reason of the style, might help to solve the problem.

The Hague

The Dutch were rather later in the field than other countries in the manufacture of porcelain. In 1775 a factory was established at the Hague, and the required capital found in shares; a German being the manager.

Though not competing with the products of France and Germany, the Hague porcelain is of good quality, and the decoration simple and unpretentious; while in the better examples, considerable taste and refinement is shown in the arrangement of design and colouring. The paste is of a good white colour, and the decoration varied, frequently representing landscapes and river views, also birds and flowers. The ware is marked with the figure

DELFT DISH, painted in blue in imitation of old Japanese Imari porcelain. XVII century. Diameter $13\frac{1}{2}$ inches, depth $1\frac{4}{5}$ inches. Franks collection, British Museum.

of a stork in blue—the arms of the Hague. It is much appreciated by the Dutch, and in some private families there are complete services for dinner, tea, and coffee, which would not be considered out of place in more imposing mansions.

Mr. Demmin, in his work, states that at one time this factory imported white porcelain of soft paste from Tournay, and that it was decorated at the Hague and the mark of the stork added. White china having to pay much less import duty than coloured, it would pay the importers to decorate this china and sell it as their own. If this is so, it shows that this factory cannot have been in a very flourishing condition. Indeed, it only lasted for ten years.

There are very few specimens of Dutch porcelain to be found at the Victoria and Albert Museum in South Kensington, and what there are will not give the collector much information or increase his appreciation; but mention may be made of a small cup and saucer of very ordinary quality, of a rather thick and yellowish paste, decorated with bunches of flowers. The saucer is marked with a stork in blue under the glaze, as it should be; but the cup has the stork marked on the glaze. The mark is dull and has not blended with the glaze. This may be an example of the imported kind decorated at home. Cup and saucer, though exactly similar, do not belong to each other (No. 270, Case 64). There is also a good specimen of a plate with blue medallions, and the centre ornamented with birds.

Arnheim

This town appears to have played a very dubious rôle in ceramic art. It is almost legendary in its reputation, for only one specimen has come down to us as an example of its pottery; and as regards porcelain, we have nothing more than rumour to satisfy us.

Amsterdam

This porcelain is known by the name of Amstel, the small river from which the capital takes its name. Its chequered career, during only forty years of existence, saw this factory removed to five different localities. It seems to have begun at a place called Overtoun; then it was taken to Weesp, not far from Amsterdam; afterwards to Loordrecht, near

DELFT PLATE, with the arms of the Elector of Brunswick. Late XVII century. Diameter $15\frac{1}{3}$ inches, depth $1\frac{4}{5}$ inches. Franks collection, British Museum.

DELFT DISH of earthenware, painted in red and gold, touched with yellow and blue in the Chinese style. XVII century. $12\frac{3}{4}$ inches by $10\frac{3}{4}$ inches. Bandinel collection, South Kensington Museum.

the town of Utrecht; finally to a suburb of Amsterdam, and it ended its career with a last removal further into the capital.

There are two specimens at South Kensington, one of Amstel and one of Loordrecht, both cups and saucers, that are not without a certain taste and refinement of style and decoration.

For some time this factory was supported by the pastor, Dr. Moll, who gave it considerable financial help. Its products are not so much esteemed by the Dutch as the Hague porcelain; still, what it has turned out is often tasteful and elegant, being of a fine paste, sometimes taking after the Dresden china, and also not unlike Sevres at times. During its occupancy of Weesp, this porcelain was marked with crossed bars and three dots in between. During Dr. Moll's management at Loordrecht its mark was "MOL," the better specimens having an additional star; and at the time the factory was at Amsterdam the mark consisted of "AMSTEL."

The decline of all these porcelain factories is no doubt attributed to the competing trade of the foreigner, especially from England; but there must have been as well a fashion or taste at this period that depreciated home products and preferred the manufacture of others. The cost may also have influenced the demand. But whatever the cause, the writer would like to bear testimony to the really extraordinary amount of English products that at some time must have been exported to Holland. Especially is this the case with furniture of the Chippendale period, and of his followers; and not only were these to be found in the houses of the wealthy, but in remote villages and farms. In the latter dwellings, also, the coloured prints of Morland were common objects hanging on the walls, the subjects—horses, pigs, and cattle—doubtless being pleasing to the bucolic mind.

English china and earthenware as well as glass were seen everywhere. Added to this comes the conservative spirit in domestic matters of the Dutch housewife, who hoards all the treasures of china in her ample cupboards, and cleans and looks after them herself. For the Dutch adage runs, "Carefulness is the mother of the china-closet;" and it may well be understood that some years ago Holland was a veritable gold-mine to the collector and the dealer—and it is not yet exhausted.

But in 1810 the French occupation took

the town of Utrecht; finally to a suburb of Amsterdam, and it ended its career with a last removal further into the capital.

There are two specimens at South Kensington, one of Amstel and one of Loordrecht, both cups and saucers, that are not without a certain taste and refinement of style and decoration.

For some time this factory was supported by the pastor, Dr. Moll, who gave it considerable financial help. Its products are not so much esteemed by the Dutch as the Hague porcelain; still, what it has turned out is often tasteful and elegant, being of a fine paste, sometimes taking after the Dresden china, and also not unlike Sevres at times. During its occupancy of Weesp, this porcelain was marked with crossed bars and three dots in between. During Dr. Moll's management at Loordrecht its mark was "MOL," the better specimens having an additional star; and at the time the factory was at Amsterdam the mark consisted of "AMSTEL."

The decline of all these porcelain factories is no doubt attributed to the competing trade of the foreigner, especially from England; but there must have been as well a fashion or taste at this period that depreciated home products and preferred the manufacture of others. The cost may also have influenced the demand. But whatever the cause, the writer would like to bear testimony to the really extraordinary amount of English products that at some time must have been exported to Holland. Especially is this the case with furniture of the Chippendale period, and of his followers; and not only were these to be found in the houses of the wealthy, but in remote villages and farms. In the latter dwellings, also, the coloured prints of Morland were common objects hanging on the walls, the subjects—horses, pigs, and cattle—doubtless being pleasing to the bucolic mind.

English china and earthenware as well as glass were seen everywhere. Added to this comes the conservative spirit in domestic matters of the Dutch housewife, who hoards all the treasures of china in her ample cupboards, and cleans and looks after them herself. For the Dutch adage runs, "Carefulness is the mother of the china-closet;" and it may well be understood that some years ago Holland was a veritable gold-mine to the collector and the dealer—and it is not yet exhausted.

But in 1810 the French occupation took

DELFT PLATE of enamelled earthenware, painted in blue with the subject of our Lord driving the buyers and sellers out of the Temple. Made by Arendt Cosijn at the sign of "The Rose." Late XVII century. Diameter $8\frac{3}{4}$ inches. South Kensington Museum.

place, and then a great change came over the country. It was Napoleon's policy to ruin English trade, and the importation of English goods was excluded.

The writer was told that at this period the china factory of Lowestoft had a large depôt for its wares at Rotterdam. The French utterly destroyed it, and the industry of Lowestoft was ruined.

CHAPTER III

POTTERY

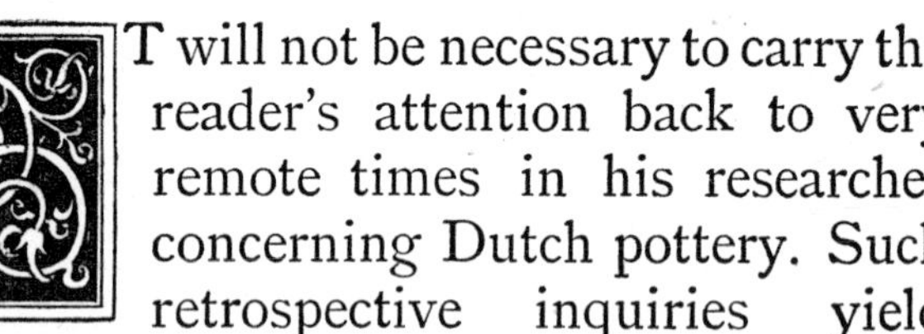

IT will not be necessary to carry the reader's attention back to very remote times in his researches concerning Dutch pottery. Such retrospective inquiries yield most unsatisfactory results, and our disappointment is only tempered by the fact that it is scarcely to be expected that dates or localities of origin would be found on fragments of pottery of the modest description and of the coarse kind made for primitive domestic use.

All peoples and tribes have begun the use of earthenware at some early period of their history; all seem to have found the necessary earth or clay wherewith to make it, and such of it as remains to excite our curiosity is only interesting when some form or shape denotes its use. A tracing or some embryo attempt at design betrays its period and the tribe or dynasty it was made by,

DELFT PLAQUE, painted in blue with view of Brussels. 12 inches by $7\frac{1}{2}$ inches. About 1670. Franks collection, British Museum.

DELFT PLATE of enamelled earthenware, painted in blue, with the subject of our Lord speaking to Zacchæus in the Sycamore tree. Made by Arendt Cosijn at the sign of "The Rose." Late XVII century. Diameter 8¾ inches. South Kensington Museum.

and the local or geographical source of its origin may be sought for in the colour or texture of the clay.

But in a small country like Holland, the vessels and utensils for ordinary use would be similar in character for a people not influenced by difference of nationality. However small, the nature of its soil, lying as it were among the branches of a great estuary coming from two central parts of Europe, would offer to the potter the necessary earth and clay to furnish his requirements in most parts of the country; and he would make his ware for local consumption—for those living in his immediate neighbourhood.

It follows that preference for any particular kind and make did not exist, nor was the name of the maker considered when the products were all the same. We are therefore left without the slightest clue as to birth of craft or craftsman. It will only have happened by a gradual process of levelling up, that a certain locality has gained a name, or repute has brought it to the notice of others. The personal influence emerged from local obscurity much later. But even so, we are far from the time when the potters' craft could give a new importance to town or village; nor was the craftsman fit to sign his name on any work as a test of skill.

Let one of the dynastic links in its history, which brought Holland eventually into the turmoils of political and religious strife, serve as our point of departure. The maze of dynastic transformations is sometimes dramatic in the extreme. After three centuries of the reign of counts, Holland, with Iceland, is joined to the countship of Hainault. After another half-century the last count dies childless, and at his death in 1354, an almost interminable series of civic commotions follow.

"Duke William of Bavaria gets himself established. He is succeeded by his brother Albert. Albert, by his son William. William, who had married Margaret of Burgundy, daughter of Philip the Bold, dies in 1417. The goodly heritage of these three Netherland provinces descends to his daughter Jacqueline—a damsel of seventeen. Little need to trace the career of this fair and ill-starred Jacqueline. Few characters of historical romance have drawn more frequent tears. The favourite heroine of ballad and drama to Netherlanders, she is endowed with the palpable form and perpetual existence of the

DELFT TEA CADDIES

Enamelled earthenware, painted with landscape and buildings in the Chinese style in yellow and green on a black ground. Marked by Lowys Fictoor at the sign of "The Double Bottle." Late XVII century. Height $3\frac{7}{8}$ inches. Collection of George Salting, Esq.

Painted in polychrome, with medallions of flowers on the edge, the rest of the surface being filled in with floral pattern on black ground. Marked by Lowys Fictoor at the sign of "The Double Bottle." Late XVII century. Height 4 inches. Collection of George Salting, Esq.

Iphigenias, Mary Stuarts, Joans of Arc, or other consecrated individualities. Exhausted and broken-hearted, after thirteen years of conflict with her own kinsman, consoled for the cowardice and brutality of three husbands by the gentle and knightly spirit of the fourth, dispossessed of her father's broad domains, degraded from the rank of sovereign to be lady forester of her own provinces by her cousin, the bad Duke of Burgundy, Philip, surnamed the Good, she dies at last, and the good cousin takes undisputed dominion of the land in 1437."

We most reluctantly leave Motley's interesting pages. It is not our purpose to follow this dynastic heritage which eventually comes to the house of Hapsburg, and finally forms one of the jewels in that resplendent crown of the Emperor Charles V.

We would rather tarry with that unfortunate princess during her voluntary incarceration at the Castle of Feylingen, midway between the Hague and Haarlem. The castle had a moat, and in the moat there were found small cylindrical jugs of grey pottery of rude workmanship. Legendary goodwill attributes these early discoveries of the potters' craft to the hand of the unhappy princess. Unfortunately other jugs of circular make have been found in other parts of the country; but we may give our sympathies the freedom desired to Jacqueline, and these jugs are still called after her, *Jacoba Kannetjes*, or, "The little jugs of Jacqueline."

But from this legendary beginning, we soon tread on firmer, but none the less uncertain, ground. We have certain localities to inquire into, but they yield us little information, or such as would satisfy us as regards their special produce; and the potters who worked there are unknown and unnamed, or if their names are mentioned, we know nothing of their work. Still, the industry cannot have been unimportant, for we shall see later from the register of names of the potters at Delft that many were strangers to the town that attracted them by its growing prosperity. The migration of craftsmen from small local potteries to establish themselves at Delft may be a reason why these unimportant places declined and passed away. So it happens that we know little of them or their origin, and they fade away in their decline, leaving us no more than the name of a town or a village, without evidence of their work, often no mark to attribute to

DELFT PLAQUE, painted in blue with view of Delft. 15½ inches wide. End of XVII century. Franks collection, British Museum.

DELFT FLOWER VASE of enamelled earthenware, painted in blue. Mark A.P. in monogram. Late XVII or early XVIII century. Height 18⅜ inches, greatest width 9 inches. South Kensington Museum.

the pottery; nor does the name of the potter, when it occurs, assist us in our difficulty.

It is not improbable that some of these potteries may have found their chief support in the making of tiles wherewith the Dutchman covered the wainscotting of his house. It would be cheaper than wood, less costly to repair, and the housewife would find it easier and quicker to clean than any other surface. The few examples still remaining of sixteenth-century houses in some of the provincial towns show us an entrance hall, the walls lined with tiles to a height of about four feet, the passages and kitchen being treated in the same way, and the farm buildings as well. The tiles were sometimes white, and sometimes decorated with patterns or figures, often with scriptural subjects in blue or violet on a white ground, generally of a childish style of drawing and conception, but often showing a certain skill, and, with a few lines and touches, giving an effect quaintly modern in its results, foreshadowing the later productions of comic illustration — little caricatures, in fact, of pikemen, musketeers, or the gentry of the period. Tiles of other colours were also made, but these are scarcer than the plain white and blue and white examples.

The first Dutch pottery as the product of an organised industry, therefore, comes to us as tiles, not only for lining the walls, but also for covering the floors and the sides of the hearth. Being of small cubic form, they have the character more of bricks than of tiles. In the British Museum there is a series of twenty-three of these bricks, in Cases 4, 5, 6, and 7, of brownish red colour, some being of a lighter shade than others, with slight indications of a worn-off glaze. The design or pattern is apparently moulded, and comes out in sharp relief, not having suffered by age. Patterns of renaissance work appear, and the decoration, which is on one side only, represents Scriptural subjects—Susannah, Samson and the foxes, St. John, St. Mark, St. Matthew, sea fights, male and female busts, the Arms of Bavaria, and of the Emperor Charles V., etc. Another larger brick, with dome-shaped top, gives the arms of the Emperor, with the date 1550, as far as can be made out.

At the Victoria and Albert Museum at South Kensington, hidden away in an obscure corner, there is a very good example of the

DELFT VASE of enamelled earthenware, painted in colours and gold. Made by Adriaen Pynacker in imitation of Japanese Imari ware. Late XVII century. Height 19 inches, diameter $9\frac{3}{4}$ inches. South Kensington Museum.

back of a hearth, a complete set of one hundred and sixty-eight bricks, with a large dome-shaped one on the top, and the date 1532. All the bricks are similar in shape and design to those at the British Museum.

A more ambitious development of the making of tiles consists in the arrangement of several placed together, forming an oblong or square, with the decoration in blue, and later in colours, of landscapes, sea-views and fleets, as well as in some instances of figure subjects, and arrangements in colour of vases holding large bunches of flowers, with birds and insects. Let into the walls, they would have the pleasing effect of pictures, a substitute for the tapestry that decorated the wealthier houses. When shown outside a building, they would commemorate some local or historical event.

Without going beyond the purpose of this chapter, namely, the consideration of the beginning of the pottery craft, another step in the development of the tile industry may be briefly referred to. I mean the increase of the size of the tile to a large panel, sometimes exceeding a yard in length and breadth. Though they occur later in its history, these panels form some of the most notable examples of the craft. The decoration and artistic treatment of these pictures show us, perhaps more than any other product of the trade, to what extent the talent of the potter had developed; in them he exhibited his national leanings and predilections uninfluenced by any foreign inspiration in form, design, or subject. The potter would also sometimes copy the pictures or drawings after great masters. We frequently come across the landscapes of Berghem, and the writer has a tile representing Rembrandt's "Woman taken in Adultery." The tile is oblong in shape, whereas the original picture, now in the National Gallery, London, is an upright.

Again, on a smaller scale, these tiles sometimes bore an escutcheon or coat-of-arms, and commemorated a wedding, or some other event of family or local interest. At a later period, the borders were sometimes ornamented in relief, and the edges were curved or scalloped. Be it noted that before these later varieties—now called plaques—were introduced, the tile was seldom signed or marked; but sometimes, when it is a work of art, the picture is signed in the corner by the artist. The absence of signature or mark in earlier specimens in no wise denotes inferiority of

DELFT PLAQUE, painted in blue. Subject, "Winter." End of XVII century. Height 15 inches. Franks collection, British Museum.

DELFT FLOWER VASE, painted in blue. Late XVII or early XVIII century. Height 12 inches. South Kensington Museum.

workmanship. The potter as yet laboured for his craft alone; the time for asserting his position among rivals had not yet come. Competition had not yet begun to influence a declining industry, and imitation had not compelled the protecting use of mark or monogram.

It will not have escaped the reader's attention that tiles of such abnormal size must have required some considerable skill in the process of baking, for any flaw or crack would have ruined the picture, the subject being painted on the clay before it was baked. The expense and risk, therefore, must have been great; and as these large tiles were only painted by apparently the most talented artists, it may be assumed that none but the wealthier would venture on the risk of sacrificing their work, unless they were tolerably certain that the potter would not spoil the tile in the oven. And if the potter himself had to run the risk, he would be likely to invite an artist of repute to decorate the tile. If successful in the baking, the product would be more valuable than if painted by an inferior artist.

It is the writer's opinion that it would not contribute much to the assistance of the collector if undue importance were given to any locality in which the pottery industry is supposed to have had its origin, nor would anything be gained by giving the names of the men of whose work we have no evidence. No specimen having as yet been proved to be attributable to the place or the craftsman with any certainty, it would be only confusing and even misleading to give particulars that down till now have only been asserted but cannot be verified.

Haarlem

Some names of potters are to be found in the archives of this town, and we have it on the authority of one of the registers at Delft that, in the year 1584, on the 1st September, a certain Herman Pietersz, a native of Haarlem, by profession a potter, was married to Anna Cornelisz. Afterwards Pietersz became one of the founders of the Guild of St. Luke, and his name appears as the first member on the Register of this corporation. And since he played a considerable part in establishing the potters' industry at Delft, we may conclude that he was a man of some experience in his craft, and deduce therefrom workmanship. The potter as yet laboured for his craft alone; the time for asserting his position among rivals had not yet come. Competition had not yet begun to influence a declining industry, and imitation had not compelled the protecting use of mark or monogram.

It will not have escaped the reader's attention that tiles of such abnormal size must have required some considerable skill in the process of baking, for any flaw or crack would have ruined the picture, the subject being painted on the clay before it was baked. The expense and risk, therefore, must have been great; and as these large tiles were only painted by apparently the most talented artists, it may be assumed that none but the wealthier would venture on the risk of sacrificing their work, unless they were tolerably certain that the potter would not spoil the tile in the oven. And if the potter himself had to run the risk, he would be likely to invite an artist of repute to decorate the tile. If successful in the baking, the product would be more valuable than if painted by an inferior artist.

It is the writer's opinion that it would not contribute much to the assistance of the collector if undue importance were given to any locality in which the pottery industry is supposed to have had its origin, nor would anything be gained by giving the names of the men of whose work we have no evidence. No specimen having as yet been proved to be attributable to the place or the craftsman with any certainty, it would be only confusing and even misleading to give particulars that down till now have only been asserted but cannot be verified.

Haarlem

Some names of potters are to be found in the archives of this town, and we have it on the authority of one of the registers at Delft that, in the year 1584, on the 1st September, a certain Herman Pietersz, a native of Haarlem, by profession a potter, was married to Anna Cornelisz. Afterwards Pietersz became one of the founders of the Guild of St. Luke, and his name appears as the first member on the Register of this corporation. And since he played a considerable part in establishing the potters' industry at Delft, we may conclude that he was a man of some experience in his craft, and deduce therefrom

DELFT WIG STAND of enamelled earthenware, painted in blue and manganese in the Chinese style. Late XVII century. Height $7\frac{1}{4}$ inches. South Kensington Museum.

that the industry at Haarlem cannot have been insignificant.

Arnheim

A single specimen from this town affords the only clue of the existence of a pottery there by having its name on the back. It is in the collection of Mr. Evenepoel at Brussels, in the form of a plaque decorated with figure subjects. In addition it has the mark of a cock, but this latter mark complicates the question of origin, for a factory at Amsterdam is also known to have used the mark of a cock.

Amsterdam

A few specimens, marked with a cock, are attributed to this town. It is supposed that the owner of this factory also had one at Arnheim, and this might perhaps explain the confusion.

Utrecht

A tile pottery of the ordinary kind existed in this town, but there is nothing to bring it more prominently to notice than the usual trade article still in use in the latter half of the eighteenth century.

Rotterdam

This town can certainly boast of having produced a man of talent whose name and work are beyond dispute. The first time his name occurs is as a worker at the pottery called "The Star," at Delft, during the period it was held by Cornelis de Berg. Both the master and his factory are well known, and some fine specimens of Delft ware came from there. A plaque with circular corners, bearing medallions of male figures enclosed by rich borders, all worked in blue, surround a central figure representing a garden scene where people are seated dining at two tables. This specimen is marked with the initials of the master, and the mark of his pottery—C.B. and the star; but in addition it has the full name, countersigned as foreman, of I AALMIS, 1731.

These are his credentials to subsequent fame as a potter after he left Delft and went to Rotterdam, where he is supposed to have set up a tile factory, profiting, no doubt, by his experience at "The Star" at Delft.

DELFT JAR of enamelled earthenware, painted in blue in the Chinese style. The mark is in simulated Chinese characters. Made by Martinus Gouda at the sign of "The Roman." Late XVII century Height $7\frac{1}{4}$ inches. Collection of George Salting, Esq.

DELFT SALAD BOWL of enamelled earthenware, painted in colours and gold in the Chinese style. Late XVII or early XVIII century. Width 8⅝ inches, depth 3⅛ inches Collection of George Salting, Esq.

Of his work at Rotterdam, we have four large picture subjects representing the seasons, each consisting of forty-eight tiles measuring together 31 inches by 41. They are signed with his name and that of the town.

Some years ago the writer was fortunate enough to come across an oblong plaque in an oak frame, signed AALMIS. The subject represented a courtyard with clipped hedges and trees, with the figure of the prodigal son on horseback leaving the paternal home. The father bids him farewell, and his mother is weeping, while other figures stand by. In the middle distance is his servant, also on horseback, with saddle-bags. All are dressed in the costume of the period in which the potter lived.

CHAPTER IV

DELFT

HERE is little to tempt the traveller, on his way from Rotterdam to the Hague, to break his journey at Delft. The Royal mausoleum and the tomb of Admiral van Tromp in the church will hardly compensate for the delay. A few local industries, a university, and a small garrison give a little life to a place that is otherwise dull, except on market-days, when the country folk come in to sell their dairy produce, and take back with them the necessaries of ordinary life. A quiet, cheerful, yet somewhat drowsy little city. The placid canals, by which it is intersected, are planted with trees, and along these watery highways the traffic of the place glides along noiselessly. The streets are clean and airy, the houses are well built, the whole aspect of the place comfortable and thriving.

DELFT PLATE, of enamelled earthenware, painted in polychrome on a black ground. Late XVII or early XVIII century. Diameter 9 inches. Fétis collection, South Kensington Museum.

It forms a link on the rail and road and canal that run from south to north through the two provinces of Holland, through an endless plain of pasture land, which in summer is dotted with thousands of black and white cattle, with here and there the steep roofs of the thatched farms, and beyond the steeple of a distant church.

Delft's principal claim to history is that it was for a short time the residence of William the Silent; and here the father of his people met his death on July 10, 1584, by the hand of the assassin.

But it was a town of importance even before that. Orange dwelt there. Like many another city of the lowlands, it owed its prosperity to some local industry, and for many years Delft was celebrated for its weaving of woollen cloth, while the number and reputation of its breweries was considerable. About a third of the town was given up to this latter industry, and it may be readily understood that the number of people employed, together with the traffic and trade in grain, hops, and wood, and the trade of the coopers, besides many secondary employments, made it a prosperous city in those days. It was walled, moated, and fortified, and therefore offered a more secure seat of Government than the neighbouring town of the Hague, which was but an open burgh. Two destructive fires and a gunpowder explosion occurring in the years 1536, 1618, and 1654, each time laid half the town in ruins; but the place was speedily rebuilt, and its prosperity seemed only to revive and increase after each disaster.

The part that the Netherlands played on the political stage of Europe in the sixteenth century entitled its Prince and his Government to the consideration of the most powerful of its rivals; and when Orange came to live at Delft, though his court was of modest extent, and he and his family lived a frugal life, he hospitably entertained the many missions and embassies that frequently sought his presence. And a mission in those days consisted not only of the chief and his secretary, but also of numerous advisers and councillors, of a host of servants, lacqueys, and retainers, with carriages and horses, prepared to make a lengthy sojourn while the tedious process of diplomatic entanglements was slowly unravelled.

With the advent of the Prince and the foreign missions, with their extensive retinue of servants, came increased wealth on the top

DELFT PLAQUE of earthenware, painted in blue camaieu. Abraham and the Angels. XVII or XVIII century. 22½ inches by 17¾ inches. Bandinel collection, South Kensington Museum.

DELFT PLATE of enamelled earthenware, painted with a Chinese landscape in green and yellow on a black ground. Late XVII or early XVIII century. Diameter $8\frac{7}{8}$ inches. Fétis collection, South Kensington Museum.

of Delft's own commercial and industrial prosperity. It did more; it brought the cultivation of artistic feeling and luxury, and a number of distinguished men of foreign culture and tastes—rich, sumptuous, money-spending, arrayed in costly brocades, moving in elegant carriages; notables and magistrates from neighbouring provinces and towns—all with a train of officialdom pertaining to their rank, with the strict precedence and etiquette, and the ceremonies of the times.

New houses and mansions were built, and decorated with a taste and luxury unknown to the patrician weaver and brewer. The windows were jewelled with coloured glass, the oak panels and staircases were embellished with wood-carving, sculpture decorated the chimney-pieces, and tapestry—already famous for the excellence of its embroidery and the beauty of its colours, and its rich designs by artists of renown—graced the walls. Noble cabinets and cupboards, in carved and inlaid woods, furnished the apartments; sumptuous chairs, upholstered in costly tapestry, or covered with golden leather, surrounded the table; and gold and silver plate, instead of pewter, graced the board, which included among its dainties the delicacies of the tropics and of the spice islands. In a few years quite a number of new arts and crafts were added to the more solid and substantial wealth of industry and trade.

With the death of Orange, and the flinging off of the yoke of Spanish cppression by the surrounding country, the Court, moved by a feeling of security, changed to the Hague; and although Delft may have lost some of the material advantages belonging to the presence of the Prince and Court, it soon recovered itself by fresh commercial enterprise.

Like several other towns in Holland, it established a chamber of commerce of the renowned East India Company. Holland's fleet, with its great admiral, van Tromp, and the more reckless "beggars of the sea," as these heroes called themselves, had swept the seas of all rivals, and the way was now open to waylay the Spanish galleons on the return home with their silver freights from Peru; and the Spanish heritage of Portuguese enterprise in the east was an alluring object for conquest and plunder. But culture and art were already influencing the town's trend towards progress and improvement.

Among the many more or less illustrious names that figured in these times as citizens

DELFT PLAQUE of enamelled earthenware, painted in polychrome. Late XVII or early XVIII century. $14\frac{3}{4}$ inches by $12\frac{1}{2}$ inches. Fétis collection, South Kensington Museum.

of Delft may be mentioned the great Admiral van Tromp, and his more reckless associate, the ready Piet Hein-Grotius, the eminent statesman and jurist, and Leeuwenhock the savant. Among painters, Miereveldt, Pieter de Hoogh and van der Meer are names that any town might well be proud of; and in many of the beershops Jan Steen must have made his humorous studies of the Dutchman in his more boisterous and convivial moments of relaxation.

In addition to the industries that belonged to so prosperous a town as Delft, the potter's trade existed as well, for making jugs and beakers wherewith to drink the beer that flowed so copiously; and that the ruder potters' craft should develop into a better kind is only natural, when we consider the change that was coming over the whole community.

What is surprising is, that it should have reached such an eminence of refinement and taste, and that its production should have continued for well nigh two centuries.

The beginning of the potter's history has long remained obscure. The first to attempt a serious account was Mr. Demmin, a German, who published a three-volume work in French (1861) on porcelain and earthenware in general, and in one of these volumes he devotes a considerable space to the industry in Holland. But his conclusions proved unreliable, and he assumed origins and dates that had no sounder base than the figures and numerals on the specimens he had collected.

In 1873 there appeared the French work by M. Jacquemart, treating of porcelain and pottery in general, including Holland.

It remained to that eminent French art critic, M. Henri Havard, to unfold a perspective of all that was necessary in order to learn the complete history of Delft pottery (1878). In a handsome volume, beautifully illustrated, and written in the charming style which French art-criticism may claim as peculiarly its own, he lays before the readers a complete history, worked out in most interesting detail, and he modestly informs us that he can carry us no further back, for the logical reason that calamities of fire and explosion had destroyed all previous records and parchments. Moreover, neglect on the part of the authorities, who in those days in Delft, as nearly everywhere else in other countries, were quite unaware of the value of the precious documents in their keeping, so interesting to

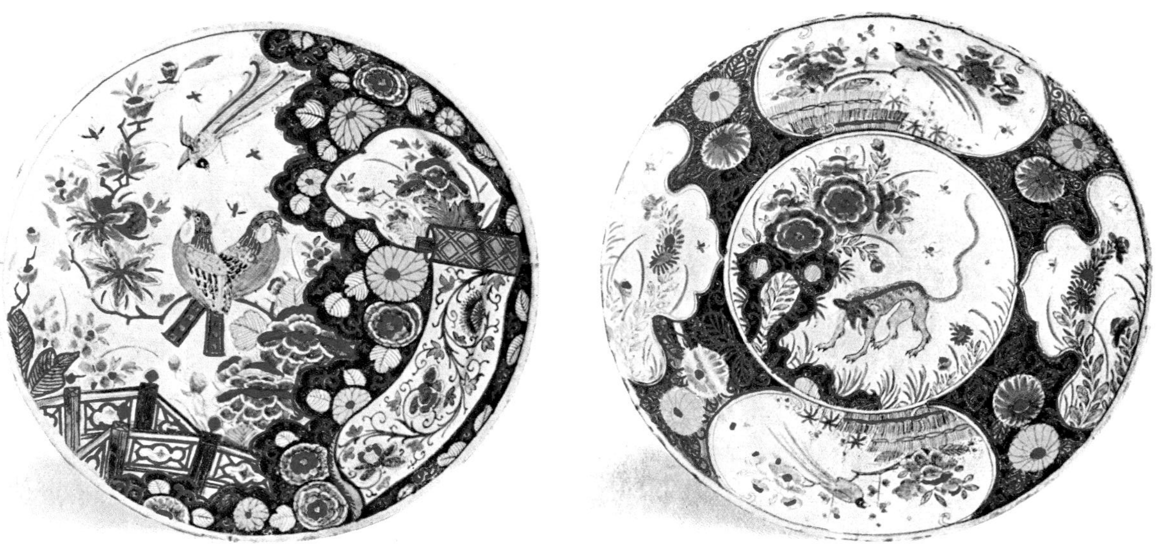

PLATE, enamelled earthenware of Delft, painted in polychrome, enriched with gold with a Japanese design. Mark of Augestijn Reygensbergh, second half of XVII century. Diameter $8\frac{7}{8}$ inches. Fétis collection, South Kensington Museum.

PLATE, painted in red, blue, green, black, and gold in imitation of Japanese Imari ware. Mark of Augestijn Reygensbergh. Late XVII century. Diameter $8\frac{1}{4}$ inches. In the collection of George Salting, Esq.

posterity, was another factor in the destruction of records.

But what more can the inquirer desire when M. Havard proves by the register of births, deaths, and marriages that on September 1, 1584, there were married Herman Pietersz, *potter*, living in Delft, widower of Haarlem, to Anna Cornelisz, spinster, of Delft; while, among all the eighteen thousand entries, this is the only one in which it is stated that the man's trade was a potter. Here we have a beginning.

But he was more than a potter. He appears to have been a man of business as well—of some considerable fortune—for at one time he was the owner of three houses in the town. His is the first name, as already stated, on the Register of the Guild of St. Luke, and no doubt he also assisted in founding the Guild. Only a very few specimens of his work are now in existence, but such as they are, with the potter's name and the dates, they furnish an authentic and reliable beginning to the history of Delft's pottery industry.

Taking him, therefore, as we find him, we may assume that a skilled workman, a stranger from a neighbouring town, was an early, if not the first, beginner of an industry that was soon to develop its name even beyond the frontiers, and cause considerable jealousy in the trade of other countries.

As we shall see at a later stage, a considerable number of these potters, when they joined the Guild, described themselves as "strangers." The list includes two or three Englishmen, soldiers by profession, who gave up the pike for the moulder's tools; but, judging from the names, nearly all were Dutchmen. The craft of the potter outside Delft must have been of some importance at this period (though we unfortunately know but little about it), for if they had been incapable workmen these new-comers would not have been admitted into the Guild. It also appears that the industry at Delft was increasing, while declining in other parts of the country, which would account for the scarcity of examples of ware from other districts.

M. Havard's researches brought him to the discovery of a long list of all the potters, the names of their apprentices, foremen, and factories, with the marks and signs belonging to each. These valuable documents may now be seen and investigated by all who choose to

DELFT PLAQUE of enamelled earthenware, with raised border painted in polychrome with flowers and a bird on a black background, the border veined with yellow. Late XVII or early XVIII century. 10 inches by $7\frac{3}{4}$ inches. Fétis collection, South Kensington Museum.

inquire; but to save the trouble and labour, it would be wiser to purchase M. Havard's book. To the serious collector it is simply indispensable.

Soon after the marriage of Herman Pietersz another curious discovery is made. On the register of the year 1600 one Hendrick Johansz qualifies as vendor of potters' earth. This trade was unknown before, but it came into existence owing to the necessity of importing certain clays from other places for mixture in the making of the finer article.

CHAPTER V

THE GUILD OF ST. LUKE

AMONG the few documents referring to the potter's trade in Holland that have been preserved, the most interesting is the deed constituting the Guild of St. Luke, which was founded some time anterior to 1611. The Guild was a more exclusive corporation than any that had previously existed among ordinary workmen, and it embraced the more skilled and talented artisans of the different arts and crafts of Delft. It contained eight specified crafts. First, painters of all kinds; secondly, stainers of glass and engravers, with the glass-makers; thirdly, potters; fourthly, embroiderers and the weavers of tapestry; fifthly, sculptors and carvers; sixthly, sheath or scabbard makers; seventhly, art printers and booksellers; and eighthly, dealers in paintings and engravings.

It further elected its deans and masters,

DELFT JAR of enamelled earthenware, painted with flowers, birds, and insects in yellow on an olive green ground. It has the mark of Lucas van Dale. Late XVII or early XVIII century. Height $10\frac{1}{4}$ inches, diameter 7 inches. Fétis collection, South Kensington Museum.

DELFT VASE, painted in blue in imitation of Chinese porcelain. Mark A.K. in monogram. XVII or XVIII century. Height 10½ inches. South Kensington Museum.

who retired by rotation, and they were not eligible for re-election until three years later. It made its own rules and regulations, was a board of selection and appointment for apprentices, who had to serve for six years, it arranged a scale of fines and awards, was a jury of approval of diploma work for the degree of mastership; and, finally, among many other rules, the members formed a trusteeship of the sick funds and old age pensions.

This powerful and influential corporation, very jealous of its own rights, very particular and exacting in carrying out and enforcing its privileges and penalties, but supporting and encouraging its members, increased and flourished for nearly two centuries; then it languished, changes came of taste and fashion, the work deteriorated, competition and artificial protection succeeded. The workers scattered, until finally, in 1833, for lack of members, it ceased to exist.

It may be of interest to give the names of the first members: first, Herman Pietersz; second, Pauwels Bourseth; third, Cornelis Rochusz van der Hoeven; fourth, Egbert Huygens; fifth, Michiel Noutsz; sixth, Thomes Jansz; seventh, Abraham Davitsz; and eighth, Symon Thonisz.

The strange terminal of the letter "z" in many of these names at this time means *zoon* or son, the same as occurs in English names, for people were only known by their Christian names. Later they took a surname, their profession or trade, and often the place they came from—such as in Dutch van der Hoeven, or van Alphen.

Naturally the potters' industry was not established at once: it had its uncertain and mysterious birth, without official registration, and no godparents to stand as sponsor for its future conduct or good behaviour. It will also have found some difficulty in its first attempt at progress, and awkwardness and clumsiness may well have been the sign previous to emancipation. And we have to consider the material that the ware was made of as well as the making; then the process of manufacture which would have to be used for any change of form or improvement in design, the fancy and the fashion that would control demand and influence supply, the decoration and embellishment that brought forth an artist of repute.

No doubt there were moderns in those days, too, who startled the academicians, and there were rivalries and jealousies; and then

DELFT FLOWER VASE, painted in blue. Marked A.K. in monogram. Late XVII or early XVIII century. Height $10\frac{3}{4}$ inches. Franks collection, British Museum.

it was that they began to sign their work and to use the trade-marks of their shops. Great men came to the front, and others dropped behind. The majority exhausted their ideas by repetition and imitation, some showed themselves eccentrics, and a few passed their well-known names on to posterity—and their work is often worth its weight in gold.

The first potters who made the necessary articles for daily life will, no doubt, have found sufficient clay in the immediate neighbourhood; but when the *Plateel Bakker* (potter baker) began to try his hand and indulge his fancy at better work, he had to call in the help of the *Potaarde Verkooper*, the seller of clay. Finding that the coarser and rougher earth, which baked into a heavy yellow brown substance, could be greatly improved by a mixture with other clays imported from the banks of the Icheld in Belgium, and the Ruhr in Germany, and turned into a malleable biscuit-coloured paste approaching white, wonderfully light in weight, and allowing of its being worked into surprising thinness, a future was opened to the enterprising potter that caused him to look round for another craftsman, the *Plateel Draaier*, or potter turner, who could turn and twist the newly discovered clay into any shape and form that appealed to the taste or fancy of the purchaser. We can imagine the proceeding and realize the success. It was not long before another craftsman joined the original trio, and the *Plateel Schilder*, or potter painter, who was now to paint the smooth creamy surface, had an endless path opened out before him, where all his fancy of combining colours with intricate design could run riot, if he were not satisfied with the more sober decoration in monochrome of blue, or cultivate his artistic feelings in the rendering of pure landscape or domestic scenes, enlivened by figures ; and so well did this new combination succeed that, proud of the position acquired, he called his house a *Porselein Fabriek*, a porcelain factory.

The reader will remember that the Guild of St. Luke included painters of all kinds, and at the beginning of its corporate duties, when the members were fewer in number than later, no doubt the various eight lodges were brought into closer contact with each other than they would have been had no guild existed, perhaps intimately enough to influence each other's work or business. We may assume that the work of the potter as a member of the guild differed in no wise from

PLATE, painted in red, blue, green, black, and gold, in imitation of Chinese porcelain. Late XVII or early XVIII century. Diameter $8\frac{1}{4}$ inches. Collection of George Salting, Esq.

SHOE, painted in blue. Late XVII or early XVIII century. Height $4\frac{5}{8}$ inches. Collection of George Salting, Esq.

the work of the outsider, and that any attempt at decoration was of the most primitive order —just a few lines, or a pattern traced with a sharp instrument on the yielding unbaked clay, very likely without any pigment. In looking down the long list of names of the potter's trade, and there are over seven hundred, all members of the guild, we see that it was only some years later that the qualifying profession is mentioned as potter-painter, the previous ones being potter-baker only; and again, some years later the word shopkeeper is frequently mentioned, denoting that a shop was attached to the factory for selling the ware, and its frequent recurrence is a proof of the prosperity of the trade.

Delft being at this time such a flourishing centre of trade and commerce, we may assume that there was an export as well as an import of earthenware from other countries, for there is a marked similarity of form and decoration in the earliest specimens of manufacture of those made in Delft with others made in France and Belgium; for in all arts and crafts there are times when a sort of universal influence is at work, either progressive or retrograde, a movement that gives character to the work and defines a period.

The beginning of Delft pottery, therefore, in no wise differs from what was being done in other parts of Europe. We find extreme simplicity coupled with inexperience, or ambitions faultily carried out. The delineation of the human figure, when attempted, was out of drawing, weak and trembling in outline, and of childish conception. Or again, one finds the most extravagant grouping and mixture of crowds of figures, jostling and pushing in utter confusion, covering the whole surface of a dish, but enclosed in a wreath or border; and of a wealth of detail consisting of foliage, flowers, fruit, cherubs, and horns of plenty, all in monochrome of blue with rarely any other colour, but sometimes with the figures outlined in a darker shade.

But before proceeding any further, we have now reached a stage in the history of Delft pottery at which we find ourselves in the presence of certain evidence and facts, and certain fields open to conjecture, which it will be advisable to sift and explore in order to avoid confusion.

The conjectural is when and where to place the beginning of the industry from the artistic point of view. And let us commence

DELFT TEAPOT of enamelled earthenware. Painted in polychrome with Chinese landscape and flowers on a black ground. It has the mark of Lowys Fictoor. Late XVII or early XVIII century. Height $5\frac{1}{2}$ inches, extreme length $7\frac{1}{8}$ inches. Fétis collection, South Kensington Museum.

with the decorative part, for this and the modelling proceed on such parallel lines that unless we keep the two apart we shall be wandering continually from one line to another.

It was several years later that men of better talent joined the Guild. Many of them, some of whom became later most important producers, came from other towns; some were painters by profession, and joined as partners the owners of already established factories. But if they were painters who had succeeded on panel or canvas, they found it quite a different matter to paint on the clay. It follows, therefore, that the rude potter could not draw, and the artist's attempts to paint on clay were mere tentative essays.

Earthenware, china, or porcelain was at its birth for general use in daily life.

A glimpse into the more domestic scenes of social and courtly history, corroborated by the evidence of contemporary art, exhibits the banqueting hall with walls hung with tapestry and the table set out with costly plate; the humbler dwelling showing us bare walls and a goblet and platters of pewter. The use of earthenware is in its infancy; but with progress and wealth, the lower class copies its master. As a new industry, the produce is costly and not within the reach of all; but some may be able to acquire and use it as an approach to what his betters possess, a substitute for something beyond his means. As a novelty, it stimulates the desire of possession; but the process being as yet costly, it cannot be turned to domestic or popular use. It is still exclusive, and therefore ornamental or decorative. As such, and in the shape of tiles, it is a cheaper substitute for marble wherewith to line the walls of the entrance or hall; in larger form and decorated in blue or colours, and in an oak frame, it may ornament a bare wall instead of pictures or prints; or the potter will, in his first attempts, mould and turn his clay into the shape of a large dish, whereon the rich man has his food served up. If the potter's partner happens to be a painter, the latter will also turn to the rich man's home for hints and ideas; he may carry out in blue colour the repoussé design of a silver dish, or he may copy a scene from some costly piece of tapestry and surround it with a rich border of foliage, fruit, and flowers. A bit of renaissance work may fall into his hands suggesting a wealth of ideas,

DELFT JAR WITH COVER, painted with birds and flowers in blue on white ground in the Chinese style. XVII or early XVIII century. Height $17\frac{5}{8}$ inches, diameter $11\frac{1}{2}$ inches. South Kensington Museum.

BACK OF A BRUSH of enamelled earthenware, painted in yellow on a black ground. Late XVII or early XVIII century. $5\frac{1}{2}$ inches by $3\frac{1}{2}$ inches. Fétis collection, South Kensington Museum.

quite beyond his powers of carrying out. The printing of the Bible is also a novelty; a copy is perhaps beyond his means of purchase, but he has long heard of the stories and they appeal to his imagination. He is most ambitious to depict some of those thrilling scenes, but his efforts are primitive; he thinks parochially, it is impossible for him to have the sense of the Eastern form, or the dress of the subject, and he renders the scene as he might observe it from his window. If he is a Catholic, he will attempt a very harrowing Passion Play on clay, appealing to the morbid feelings of his friends or client. If he be a Protestant, he will choose some episodes from the Old Testament, such, for instance, as Adam and Eve with the serpent, Abraham's sacrifice, and Moses on the Mount, or he will copy some work by Goltzius or other graver of repute or fashion.

To propitiate a patron, he may make a plaque or dish with the burgess' newly adopted coat of arms, or he may receive an order to design some commemorative piece for the birth or birthday of a member of some patrician family, with the full name and age of the celebrant, and the date all set out on it.

With work and experience the hand of the artist becomes more facile, and the potter finds that he can mix and turn his clay in every shape and form desired; and when the industry is at the point of reaching a state of wonderful prosperity an event of far-reaching importance occurs.

DELFT COVERED VASE of enamelled earthenware, with embossed scrolls, and painted with a Chinese female figure and flowers in polychrome on a turquoise ground. Late XVII or early XVIII century. Height $6\frac{1}{4}$ inches. Fétis collection, South Kensington Museum.

CHAPTER VI

THE RISE AND FALL

EFERENCE has already been made to Delft being one of the branches of the celebrated East India Company. The seas being now clear, the Dutchman sought his way to the remoter corners of the East, where the Portuguese had preceded him. What he took out with him on these trade ventures is difficult to say, but in exchange and barter he will have returned with the produce of those distant lands, including those of the far-famed spice islands, where the legendary aroma of the plantations was wafted over the sea before the islands were reached.

All those towns in Holland connected with the company were on rivers or estuaries, or on that inland sea called the Zuider Zee; and these northern towns, Amsterdam, Hoorn,

Enkhuizen, and Medenblik were all of equal importance in those days.* It is hard to realize that Enkhuizen stretched over what are now extensive and productive fields, producing corn, carraway seed, onions, and cauliflowers ; and that Amsterdam, as a trading port, would certainly not have retained its importance but for the canals that cut through the mainland, enabling its merchandise to reach the sea. The other towns were of much more importance than they are now. The cause of their decline was the improvement and increased size of the ships, which, owing to their deeper draught, were unable to navigate the shallow waters of the Zuider Zee, upon which the towns stood. Some venerable buildings exist to this day with the arms and monogram of the Company "O.I.C." still embedded in the walls of the warehouses, where frequently, even now, pepper corns are found in the crevices of the floors and timbers that have remained hidden there all these long years.

Though not on either river or sea, Delft had its port close by on the Maas, called

* See Henri Havard's interesting and entertaining book, "Les Villes Mortes."

DELFT PLAQUE, painted in blue. Christ before Caiaphas. By P. Vizeer. Height $11\frac{1}{4}$ inches. Dated 1768. Franks collection, British Museum.

DELFT PLAQUE, painted in blue. The Flagellation. By P. Vizeer. Height $11\frac{1}{2}$ inches. Dated 1769. Franks collection, British Museum.

Delftshaven, and the goods and wares of its company were carried by inland craft along the canal that connects the two towns.

The trade adventurer was never at a loss to discover some new article suitable for exchange and barter, and he often brought back from his voyages samples of the products of the peoples with whom he had been trading. Among the varied cargo that the Dutchman carried on his homeward journey, not the least important was the ceramic ware of China and Japan—wonderful creations of Oriental art, made of a material that was then unknown in Europe.

Here was an unexpected intrusion into the potter's domain, but the threatened foreign invasion was happily only a false alarm. It became, wonderful to relate, an alliance, reciprocally and faithfully carried out on both sides. In the first place, the foreign article was of such a costly nature that it put itself beyond the reach of any purchaser but the most wealthy. The clay it was made of was quite unknown, such brightness had never been seen before, and its strength and firmness were surprising. It was as white as snow and as smooth as marble. The colours, too, were amazing; the flaked or mottled blue, as well as the strange combinations and schemes of colouring, came as a revelation to the potter.

So the Dutchman, after his first surprise, sat down quickly and proceeded to copy the new models; and being of a temperament and character that revels in minute detail and closely finished work, he copied all that came in shape and form, in colour, and design, and pattern so closely and correctly that at a short distance there was nothing to choose between his work and the original. In glaze, in colour, in shape, in form, there was no difference, but he could not make the paste, for he had not got the clay. He covered his own material so artfully, however, that the deception was complete. But the process of manufacture was expensive, and his work remained ornamental and decorative, and consequently only for the few. Those huge ribbed and channelled vases of creamy white, with designs that appear borrowed from costly and delicate silk and woollen materials, with schemes of colouring in which the blue, red, and gold were brought into the most harmonious blendings, could find a suitable and worthy place only in the corners of banqueting halls, or beside the high chimney piece of the most

DELFT BOWL, painted in blue. Circa 1700. Diameter $8\frac{1}{2}$ inches, depth $3\frac{1}{3}$ inches. Franks collection, British Museum.

opulent. The high cylindrical vases or gourd-shaped bottles, with long necks worked out in blue, with landscape or tall draped figures, or warriors with shields painted upon them, found fitting resting places on the side-boards of the wealthy. The curious sets of three, five, or even seven jars and goblets graced the tops of cabinets which held within their glazed doors the choicest specimens that virtuoso could bring together of all the multitude of cups and saucers, teapots, dishes, plates, and figures that had been hoarded by his Chinese rival collector centuries before.

The potter had now reached the apogee of his career. He could make and decorate the imitation ware of China and Japan with a skill and finish that equalled the craft and cunning of the Oriental. He could turn out large plaques, painted in blue, of the most charming landscapes and scenes of towns and rural life—veritable pictures. He even attempted portraiture in blue monochrome with great success, as well as scenes borrowed from prints and engravings, sometimes modifying the composition to suit an upright plaque or the circular form of a large dish.

The potter and his fellow craftsman, the potter-painter, were on the flood of the spring-tide that has carried their art and craft beyond any of its kind in Europe. But not content with this enviable position, they now started on quite a different tack, and on this long course the tide turned, and the ebb carried them further and further back.

It was an ingenious idea to send out to China samples of Dutch ware, such as were now in use, and get the Chinese to copy these models in their superior clay. This was the reciprocity to the Chinaman's export of his own produce. And this keenness for trade was carried yet another step further when the Dutchman sent his potter's ware to be wholly or partly decorated by the Chinaman.

But in doing this the potter overreached himself; for if he did part of the decoration, and the Chinaman the rest, it followed naturally that there would be two processes in the baking, in which one colouring would be under, or amalgamated with the glaze, and the other would be on the surface, and would appear as later work painted on the glaze, which indeed it was.

Anyhow, it did not matter so long as trade improved and brought in money. The art now became a trade; the produce was no longer exclusive, artistic, and ornamental; it

DELFT PLATE, one of a set of twelve, painted with the signs of the Zodiac in blue by Sir James Thornhill in 1711. Afterwards the property of his daughter, Mrs. Hogarth, and later of Horace Walpole. Diameter $8\frac{1}{2}$ inches. Franks collection, British Museum.

DELFT BOTTLE of enamelled earthenware, painted in blue. Mark of Anthoni Kruisweg. 1759–64. Height 12 inches. Fétis collection, South Kensington Museum.

came within the reach of all. Hitherto he had confined his efforts to borrowing ideas from the established art of others, whether silversmith, weaver of tapestry, painter, or etcher, and he had been most successful in imitating the wonderful imports from the East. But now his fancy turned more to things of domestic use. The potter's trade became popular—gradually, of course. Several factories and many men continued to carry out the craft on the old-established lines. But prosperity produced competition, and even imitation. The monogram with which the artist signed his finished work became a trade-mark, and the name of the factory had to be added, or he delegated this to a foreman or licensed overseer, and a numeral was often added, probably denoting the number of the order.

Another cause of decline, owing to the double process of decorating and baking, was due to the fact that the skilled artisan was supplanted by a quite inferior workman, and new rules had to be made in the Guild of St. Luke in order, by means of fines, to rectify this evil. It may be easily understood that decorating on the unbaked clay was a skilful process, requiring a practical hand as well as dexterity in execution. There could be no retracing or alteration, and a mistake could not be corrected; but when the clay was once baked with its blue border or design, and an outline given of the proposed figures, these could afterwards be filled in with colour by any ordinary workman. The surface no longer absorbed the paint; it was hard and smooth, and the painting could be changed, corrected, or wiped out. So the skilful hand lost his employment and his wages, and frequently had to apply to the authorities for charity.

And others allowed the old fame of quality to slip away and turn their efforts to the produce of quantity. Taste, as well as fashion and a sense of luxury and comfort, may have contributed to this result. We must remember that earthenware was a material that lent itself to the production of articles which were formerly only within the reach of the wealthy, such as plates, cups and saucers, bowls, and mugs. We now get teapots, coffee-pots, milk-jugs, sugar-basins. Then came soup and vegetable tureens, butter-bowls, oyster-platters, pancake-dishes, oil and vinegar stands, salt-cellars, and pepper-castors, vases and bottles for the chemist to hold his drugs, and for the tobacconist to keep his tobacco and snuff, with

DELFT PLAQUE of enamelled earthenware painted in blue. Subject, "The Holy Family." XVIII century. $20\frac{1}{2}$ inches by $17\frac{3}{4}$ inches. Bandinel collection, South Kensington Museum.

the various names painted on the side. Perforated square boxes, holding a small vessel containing live peat, on which the housewife kept her stockinged feet warm ; little boxes, in the form of prayer-books, for holding hot water, and carried in the muff as hand-warmer ; hot-water bottles on their stands ; spittoons, elaborately worked, and decorated bird-cages ; cisterns containing water, made to hang on the wall for washing hands ; and, lastly, to carry the fancy to its highest flight, exact copies of violins, decorated with figure-subjects in blue, of which four authentic examples only are really known.

As regards these four violins, M. Henri Havard attributes them to four members of the van der Hoeven family—people of good position in Delft, and all master-potters of the Guild of St. Luke. He also attributes to one of them a plate showing a coat-of-arms of three violins, which was the family's escutcheon. This is a happy idea, and M. Havard may be right ; at all events, there is nothing to gainsay his assumption. A similar plate may be seen in the British Museum.

Many plates, both blue and coloured, and also plaques were made at Delft showing coats-of-arms, some beautifully executed and coloured. Examples of these may be seen in Mr. George Salting's collection at the Victoria and Albert Museum, and also at the British Museum. It was not at Delft alone that these armorial bearings were illustrated; we have it also on some English china, as well as on the porcelain imported from China, which also sent to Holland those fine dishes with the coats-of-arms of the Netherlands, often surrounded with beautiful borders picked out with enamel.

And when the Dutchman had exhausted all the Oriental ideas, which he had copied and imitated with a cunning worthy of the original maker, he was at a loss for novelty; he did not strike out in a new direction, or make a fresh attempt in art and skill, but contented himself with the easy produce of domestic ware. The inferior work demanded unskilled hands, and there was no inducement for taste or talent to assert itself. Competition came, notably from England, and an Englishman, a certain Captain Picardt, who was in the Dutch service, gave up the sword and bought a factory, making popular pottery, up-to-date in topical subjects, hideous produce of yellowish colour, with red figures, and mottoes favouring the house of Orange against the

DELFT SALAD DISH of enamelled earthenware, painted in polychrome. XVIII century. Diameter $15\frac{1}{4}$ inches, depth $3\frac{1}{2}$ inches. Fétis collection, South Kensington Museum.

PLAQUE, painted in polychrome, in imitation of Chinese porcelain. XVIII century. Width $10\frac{3}{4}$ inches. Collection of George Salting, Esq.

Republic. And the ware of Turner was also imported from England, and had a great sale because of its strength and ability to resist a high temperature.

There has been much exaggeration about Delft pottery. It is quite certain, however, that for a century Delft was the most important manufactory in Europe, and none other turned out such fine and handsome work; and although none could compete with it at this period, and the export trade was enormous, it cannot be denied that it was a beautiful and splendid carrying out of borrowed ideas.

The first period was taken, as mentioned before, from the possessions and treasures of the wealthiest classes. The second, or great period, from the importation of Chinese and Japanese china. The shape and form and design, and the beautiful and brilliant colours of blue, green, red, yellow, and also gold, are all taken from Oriental models. But this is also equally certain, that if not original in conception, it is quite original in execution. Although, when placed close together, it is difficult to observe the difference between the Oriental vase and the Dutch one, yet there is something that stamps the Delft specimen at once as a product entirely apart from any other European ware. This is hard to explain, and no reason can be given. The power to discriminate and recognise the difference is an acquired talent. It is an instinct, and cannot be taught, but it will come to those who have the eye and the sense for it.

One characteristic Delft pottery possesses above any other is its wonderful glaze; such brilliancy has not been obtained anywhere else. It is not the lustre of the Italian or the Hispano-moresque, nor the metallic reflections of the Persian or Rhodian; it has no suggestion of tints or hues, but is simply the transparent covering of the paste. It was owing probably to the proportion of tin used, and also perhaps to the baking; but other towns and countries used the same tin, which came from England.

It has been said that the prices obtained by the potters for their productions were enormous; but we have documentary evidence that articles which would now fetch £50 were ordered by the dozen for a few pence. The number of workers has been put at thousands, but could only have been hundreds, since the population of this whole town was only twenty-four thousand. The number of the

DELFT POTTERY CANDLESTICK, painted in blue. XVIII century. Height $5\frac{7}{8}$ inches, width of base $4\frac{1}{8}$ inches. South Kensington Museum.

factories has been stated in scores, yet it can be proved that only about thirty existed, and their names are given later. Much also has been written, almost too much, about the individual potter, of the artist as potter, and of remote dates, which have been found to be, after all, only numerals of orders. And it would be well here to indicate the curious recurrence in factories or families of potters of some trait or peculiarity—a beautiful scheme of colouring, a brilliant glaze, or some ingenious arrangement or treatment which seemed to have been long extinct and then again returns, an hereditary likeness, as it were, in factory or family of a forgotten beauty. And this recurrence continues down to the very end, when the last factory, the celebrated "Three Bells," was sold in 1850.

CHAPTER VII

MASTERS AND FACTORIES

HE reader who has followed the history of Delft pottery from the earliest beginnings, through its rise and fall, will now expect to make a closer acquaintance with the factories that produced the work, and with the names of the men who contributed to raise the craft to such a wonderful state of importance.

The list of the members of the Guild of St. Luke has fortunately escaped destruction, and it may be found and studied in the National Library at the Hague. It includes over seven hundred names, states the place of birth, gives the date of his entry into the Guild, and mastership, and generally the name of the factory he worked in, though this latter statement does not occur in the earliest entries.

But of most of these men we have the names only. Nothing can be attributed to factories has been stated in scores, yet it can be proved that only about thirty existed, and their names are given later. Much also has been written, almost too much, about the individual potter, of the artist as potter, and of remote dates, which have been found to be, after all, only numerals of orders. And it would be well here to indicate the curious recurrence in factories or families of potters of some trait or peculiarity—a beautiful scheme of colouring, a brilliant glaze, or some ingenious arrangement or treatment which seemed to have been long extinct and then again returns, an hereditary likeness, as it were, in factory or family of a forgotten beauty. And this recurrence continues down to the very end, when the last factory, the celebrated "Three Bells," was sold in 1850.

CHAPTER VII

MASTERS AND FACTORIES

HE reader who has followed the history of Delft pottery from the earliest beginnings, through its rise and fall, will now expect to make a closer acquaintance with the factories that produced the work, and with the names of the men who contributed to raise the craft to such a wonderful state of importance.

The list of the members of the Guild of St. Luke has fortunately escaped destruction, and it may be found and studied in the National Library at the Hague. It includes over seven hundred names, states the place of birth, gives the date of his entry into the Guild, and mastership, and generally the name of the factory he worked in, though this latter statement does not occur in the earliest entries.

But of most of these men we have the names only. Nothing can be attributed to

DELFT KETTLE AND STAND of enamelled earthenware, painted in blue. On the bottom of the kettle is the mark of G. Verstelle. XVIII century. Height of kettle $9\frac{1}{2}$ inches, diameter $7\frac{1}{2}$ inches; height of stand $4\frac{3}{4}$ inches. South Kensington Museum.

PLAQUE, painted in polychrome, with moulded rococo border. Middle of XVIII century. 15 inches by 11½ inches. Collection of George Salting, Esq.

them, for we have nothing to show of their work, nor do we know in which factory they worked. We propose, therefore, to omit the names of these obscure persons, to give those names only to whom we can ascribe certain work and marks, aided by a record of the factory they occupied as a guide to the attribution of any specimens which may come under the collector's notice. We have also considered it unnecessary to give the dates of marriage, the names of children, and such like details, confining ourselves to supplying the name of the master and of his factory, the marks, and descriptions of the kind of work turned out, with such details as regards character of ware, form, colour, and glaze—in fact, any broad line or peculiar trait that may be of use as a guide to the collector and student.

Illustrations are given of specimens by the principal potters, selected from the collections at the Victoria and Albert Museum, South Kensington, and the British Museum. But neither a written description nor an exact reproduction will be of so much value to a student as an examination of actual pieces of the ware. An hour's study of the abovementioned collections will give a good idea of Delft pottery, and will enable a student to understand the variety of the product, the different forms and shapes, the richness of the decoration, and the extraordinary brilliancy of the glaze. It is by seeing a quantity massed together that we are able to judge of its general effect, its character and peculiarities. Such an examination leaves a decided impression on the mind, which is more effective and lasting than the study of a single specimen at odd times.

The writer was never more impressed with this value of massed effect than when he had the pleasure of admiring, for the first time, the unique collection belonging to M. Evenepoel of Brussels, under the personal escort of the fortunate owner. It is only on such an occasion that the work of the great men is brought vividly to our notice, and we are able to draw conclusions and comparisons between their art and the personality of their craft. We can detect what the writer has allowed himself to call a "family likeness" running from the founder of a style, through his children and his sons-in-law, and continued many years later. Or we have the produce of a certain factory, where the successive masters and foremen

DELFT DISH, with portrait of the Prince of Orange, son-in-law of King George II. Date 1750. Diameter $10\frac{2}{5}$ inches. Franks collection, British Museum.

have retained the original quality of paste and harmony of colour and decoration. And again, the art that seems to have departed with the death of a master, revives a century later in the same house, leaving the collector in doubt as to the period of his specimen.

Among the more illustrious names that occur at the beginning of the history, those of Abraham de Kooge (1632) and Aelbrecht de Keizer (1642) stand out conspicuously. The former is known by his fine plaques representing landscapes, and some portraits and dishes, with commemorative names and dates, all worked in blue. The writer at one time possessed one representing "Abraham's Sacrifice." The design and drawing are by a master hand, for de Kooge qualified, on entering the Guild, as a painter in oils. The colouring is of a fine blue, and the peculiarity of his work is that the material is rather thick, though it is covered with a fine creamy paste. Both he and de Keizer were strangers to Delft. The latter was the precursor of the celebrated potter Cornelis de Keizer and the two Pynackers. His work shows a wonderful thinness and lightness of paste, especially in the charming blue he produced resembling the Oriental in design;

but his principal claim to fame was that he was the originator of those wonderful creations in coloured ware in imitation of the Chinese and Japanese, which in later years was carried out also by the great men Lowys Fictoor, Lambertus Eenhoorn, Augustein Reygensbergh, and others—all known for their glorious schemes of colouring in which blue, red, and gold predominate. Of these latter men, Lowys Fictoor (1689) and Lambertus Eenhoorn (1691) deserve special mention; for to them we owe those choice and very rare specimens of black Delft, with their wonderful glaze, decorated in Chinese style of pagodas and trees, in yellow and green. Owing to the similarity of their work of the grandest and best quality, the initials carelessly combined assume a mark or monogram most provokingly alike, and it is only by the additional mark of the foreman of the factory that the collector is able to distinguish the one from the other. Other distinguished names occur, such as two other Eenhoorns, and the Kams, of whom we know five. There were four van der Hoevens; there was Frytom, who painted beautiful plaques and plates with figures; the two Dextras; Lucas van Dale, who has

DELFT DISH of enamelled earthenware, painted in blue with a Chinese design. XVIII century. Diameter 19½ inches. Fétis collection, South Kensington Museum.

DELFT BOTTLE of double gourd shape, of enamelled earthenware, painted in blue. Marked by A. Kruisweg at the sign of "The Old Moor's Head." XVIII century. Height $12\frac{1}{4}$ inches. Collection of George Salting, Esq.

left us those rare specimens in olive-brown decorated with yellow; Leonard van Amsterdam, whose work reminds us of Dresden china, with figures and shipping, and small landscapes painted in colour on butter-bowls and the backs of brushes; whilst Verhagen took his motives from the prints of Goltzius, reviving thereby the ideas which originated with Herman Pietersz.

And when we leave the masters and turn to the factories, the history of Delft pottery loses none of its interest. The names of about thirty factories have come down to us, some of which were always fortunate in being either in possession or under control of the foremost men of the day. Others seem to have carried on a special kind of work, uniform in character, irrespective of master or foreman's influence. On many specimens we find the mark of the factory only, and we are left uncertain as to the makers or at what period they were made. Such pieces came especially from "The Peacock," "The Claw," "The Rose," "The Star," and "The Three Bells."

But we have some fine specimens from "The Rose" and "The Star," even if we are not certain about the maker. These consist of the beautiful plates in blue decoration of figure subjects—in landscape, sometimes—surrounded with charming borders of fruit and flowers. Often the pictures represent religious subjects, and are treated in a masterly way; or again, we find the signs of the Zodiac denoted in the border, and the plate is painted with seasonable landscapes of quite picturesque design.

We have the pottery called the "Greek A," which continued an artistic career worthy of the Eenhoorns and the Dextras. "The Moor's Head" was owned by Abraham de Kooge, the two Hoppesteins, and finally Verhagen.

A study of the work produced by a factory is often just as interesting as the work of the masters, since some of the potteries have throughout their career retained a personality of style and effect that might almost be attributed to an individual.

DELFT PLATE, painted with the arms of Van der Hoeve. Date about 1759. Diameter $8\frac{4}{5}$ inches. British Museum.

APPENDIX A

THE DELFT POTTERIES

De Metale Pot . .	1639.	The Metal Pot
De Griekse A . .	1645.	Alpha
De Dubbelde Schenk Kan	1648.	The Double Jug
De Paauw	1651.	The Peacock
De Klauw	1658.	The Claw
In de Porseleine Fles	1659.	The Porcelain Bottle
Het Hert	1661.	The Stag
In de Boot	1661.	The Boat
De Oude Moriaans Hooft	1661.	The Old Moor's Head
De Roos	1675.	The Rose
De Drie Klokken .	1675.	The Three Bells
In de Romeyn . .	1671.	The Roman
De Drie Porseleine Fleschen	1671.	The Three Porcelain Bottles
De Drie Astonne	1674.	The Three Cinder Tubs

De Porseleine Byl .	1679.	The Porcelain Axe
De Ster	1690.	The Star
De Wilde Man . .	1682.	The Savage
De Vergulde Blompot	1693.	The Gilt Flower Pot
In de Dissel . . .	1696.	The Axe
De Porceleine Schotel	1701.	The Porcelain Dish
Het Fortuyn . . .	1692.	The Fortune
De Vier Helden van Rome	1713.	The Four Roman Heroes
De Drie Tonnen . .	1720	The Three Tuns
De Nieuwe Moriaans Hooft	1759.	The New Moor's Head
De Twee Scheepjes .	1759.	The Two Little Boats
De Lampet Kan . .	1759.	The Jug
De Twee Wildemans	1764.	The Two Savages

SPITTOON, painted in polychrome. Second half of the XVIII century. Height 3 inches, width $4\frac{1}{4}$ inches. Collection of George Salting, Esq.

APPENDIX B

THE MEMBERS OF THE GUILD OF ST. LUKE

NLY the names of those of whom the marks are known or who have left examples of their work are given.

HERMAN PIETERSZ (1584)

A native of Haarlem. M. Havard places him as one of the founders of the potter's industry, but not much is known of his work; his name has, however, been referred to earlier in this work.

THOMES JANSZ (1611)

An Englishman; his name has been referred to already.

GERRIT HERMANSZ (1614)

A very few of the earliest specimens of Delft are supposed to be by him.

Cornelis Cornelisz (1628)

Certain specimens marked with a "C" are attributed to him.

Abraham de Kooge (1632)

A stranger. This great master has already been referred to. His plaques and dishes in blue may be considered as some of the finest early specimens of Delft. The paste is rather thick and the specimens, as a result, rather heavy, but the colouring and the glaze are very fine. His work was never signed, but the date is given in a small cartouche with the head of a cherub above.

Pieter Hieronimus van Kessel (1634)

Not much is known of his work, but he is supposed to be the founder of "The Metal Pot," and certain specimens signed with the letter "P" are attributed to him.

Lambrecht Ghisbrechts (1640)

A stranger. He is supposed to have produced models of cocks, ducks, etc., of a brilliant colouring and signed "L G."

THOMES JANSZ
1590

TOME
SWA

GERRIT HERMANSZ
1614

16 E 13 4
DEN 2 M

CORNELIS CORNELISZ
1628

C

ABRAHAM DE KOOGE
1632

P. H. VAN KESSEL
1634

P

LAMBRECHT
GHISBRECHTS
1640

LG

ISAACK JUNIUS
1640

Junius 6/16 1657

AELBRECHT
DE KEISER
1642

AK AK

GHISBRECHT
LAMBRECHTSE KRUYK
1645

GK GK

SAMUEL
VAN BERENVELT
1648

D S.K

APPENDIX

Isaack Junius (1640)

Two examples exist in blue, representing the tomb of William the Silent, and signed with Junius' name in full and the date 1657.

Aelbrecht Cornelis de Keizer (1642)

A stranger, and one of the great men. His name has already been referred to in conjunction with that of Abraham de Kooge. De Keizer's work is amongst the best of the earlier potters. Its charm is due to its extreme thinness and lightness. The writer had three plates of Oriental design in blue by de Keizer in his collection, which might have passed for the finest porcelain. De Keizer is also famous as the first to introduce the Chinese and Japanese style of modelling and decoration. In this he excelled, and this talent was handed down to his sons-in-law the Pynackers. His signature was a combined "A K."

Ghisbrecht Lambrechtse Kruyk (1645)

He may have been the founder of the celebrated pottery "Alpha," for he handed it over to his nephew van Eenhoorn in 1674. Some specimens, of a rather pale colour, with his monogram of "G K" in blue, have a distinction peculiarly their own and are easily recognized.

Samuel van Berenvelt (1648)

A stranger, supposed to be the founder of "The Double Jug"; but we cannot attribute anything to his hand, for specimens with the mark of the factory "D K" or "D S K" give us no clue to the maker.

Jan Van der Hoeve (1649)

A member of the family that made itself a name by adopting as its coat-of-arms three fiddles, as a model for their work; but of this member we have very little to show beyond his initials "V H" on some unimportant articles.

Claes Messchert and Abraham van Noorden (1651)

Founders of "The Peacock" pottery, but we cannot distinguish their work from that of successors at this factory, for the various combinations of its mark "PAAUW" give no clue to the maker.

APPENDIX

Quiring Aldersz Kleynoven (1655)

A stranger associated with some of the best masters; but although he registered his mark, forming a monogram of his three initials, nothing is known of his work.

Jeronimus van Kessel (1655)

A few coloured specimens signed "J V K" are attributed to him.

Frederick van Frytom (1658)

His work stands out from any other worker at Delft in that he did not copy the Oriental or take his ideas from the designs of other arts. His work is pure landscape painting, enlivened with figures, such as the large plaque at the Netherlands Museum at the Hague, signed with his name in full in the corner. He also painted plates of the most charming description with figures, such as the one at the British Museum.

Jan van der Houk (1659)

He began at the sign of "The Porcelain Bottle." Specimens of his work, signed with his initials, are casseroles and dishes of very brilliant colouring in the form of birds, ducks, fowls, etc.

Jan Groenlant (1660)

He is supposed to have made little busts and statuettes in coloured ware.

Joris Mes (1661)

We find him working at the sign of "The Stag." The mark of this factory occurs rather frequently on blue ware of small articles of interesting quality.

Jan van Hammen (1661)

His work is both in blue and coloured, signed with his initials "I H" and the numbers.

Jacob Wemmers Hoppestein (1661)

At the sign of "The Old Moor's Head." He seems to have carried out at this factory the excellent work begun by his predecessor Abraham de Kooge, and the produce of this factory had a high reputation. It consisted

JAN VAN DER HOEVE
1649

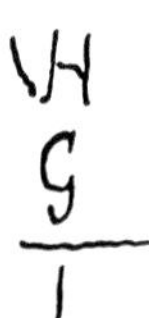

C. J. MESSCHERT
1651

D PAUW

Q. A. KLEYNOVEN
1655

J. P. VAN KESSEL
1656

A. J. DE MILDE
1658

1663 · A I ·

F. VAN FRYTOM
1658

F. V FRYTOM

J. VAN DER HOUK
1659

J. GROENLANT
1660

JORIS MES
1661

T H A R T

J. A. VAN HAMMEN
1661

H
10
12

JH
12
3

J. WEMMERS
HOPPESTEIN
1661

J. J. KULICK
1662

generally of blue decorative centres representing episodes from Roman history, surrounded by coloured borders. Examples of this kind may be seen at South Kensington and at the British Museum. His monogram consisted of an "I" through a "W," or the two letters placed together.

Jan Jansz Kulick (1662)

A stranger. Having worked under Aelbrecht de Keizer, he produced, like his master, fine specimens in imitation of Chinese and Japanese ware in blue, red, and gold. M. Havard gives his monogram, but states that he has never come across it on a piece of pottery.

Johannes Kruyck (1662)

A stranger. Some articles in blue, of good quality, and signed with the monogram "I K," are attributed to him.

Cornelis van der Hoeve (1662)

At the sign of "The Claw."

The strange mark of this factory, representing a claw, is of frequent occurrence. It is generally found on blue ware of good quality, but many of the pieces are quite unimportant.

Augestijn Reygensbergh (1663)

A stranger. He took as foreman J. J. Kulick, a former pupil of de Keizer, and his influence soon became apparent in continuing the production of those wonderful imitations of Chinese and Japanese ware in blue, red, and gold. The work of Reygensbergh is quite equal to that of any of his rivals. It consists of sets of vases and beakers, bottles, jugs, dishes, and plates. M. Havard mentions in addition plates with figures and French inscriptions. His mark is the monogram "A R."

Willem Kleftijus (1663)

A stranger. Like many another potter, his work is irregular in quality, but his coloured ware, at its best, is not unlike that made by Lambertus Eenhoorn. His monogram was a "W K," with a number.

Jan de Weert (1663)

M. Jacquemart attributes a bowl in blue, with pastoral scene, signed "I D W," to this master.

J. KRUYCK
1662

C. VAN DER HOEVE
1662

A. REYGENSBERGH
1663

W. KLEFTIJUS
1663

J. DE WEERT
1663

IDW

L. CLEFFIUS
1667

J. MES
1667

P. G. KAM
1667

C. A. DE KEIZER
1668

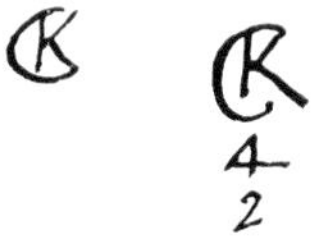

J. PIETERSZ
1668

M. B. FLYT
1669

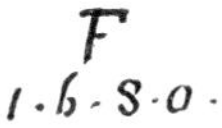

B. ROTTEWEL
1671

ARY JANSZ
1671

APPENDIX

Lambertus Cleffius (1667)

At the sign of "The Metal Pot" he advertised himself as having discovered the secret of making porcelain, but there is nothing in his work to warrant the assumption of any superiority of quality. His work is characterised by the use of a stronger shade of colour for the outline than for the ground of the design. His monogram consisted of his initials.

Johannes Mes (1667)

One of those accomplished men who produced the fine pieces in red, blue, and gold. His signature consists of a combined "MES."

Pieter Gerritsz Kam (1667)

Worked in blue, and signed with his monogram "PK."

Cornelis de Keizer (1668)

Son of the celebrated A. de Keizer. He is supposed to have worked with his two brothers-in-law, the Pynackers. A monogram composed of their united initials was deposited at the Guild, but no specimens so marked are known. Certain pieces, however, marked with his initials only exist, including some of an olive-green colour, with design traced in yellow, somewhat similar to one in the South Kensington Museum signed by Lucas van Dale.

Jan Pietersz (1668)

A stranger. He worked for a long time in the factory of the celebrated Lowys Fictoor, and signed his initials as a monogram, sometimes singly, and sometimes below those of Fictoor. His work is that of simulated Chinese decoration, which the French call cashmere. Signature " I P."

M. B. Flyt (1669)

A stranger. One or two pieces marked with an " F " are attributed to him.

Barbara Rottewel, Wife of Simon Mes (1671)

Kept a shop, where she doubtless sold the wares of her husband's factory. At all events, those pieces are marked with a sign of " The

Three Bells," and they are often met with. The colouring is blue, and the work consists of jugs, bottles, beakers, dishes, and plates of a good glaze and colour.

Ary Jansz (1671)

Certain pieces, of Chinese design in pale blue, and signed with an "A I," are attributed to him.

Martinus Gouda (1671)

At the sign of "The Roman."

Not much is known of this potter, but, fortunately, he registered his mark at the Guild, which enables us to credit him with a few specimens marked with a device of simulated Chinese characters and strange hieroglyphics. These examples are very rare. There is nothing remarkable about the blue decoration. The little vase in the Salting collection, which formerly belonged to the present writer, gives a fair idea of his work. Another example in olive-green, with yellow decoration, belonging to Mr. Evenepoel, of Brussels, shows that he attempted work in colours.

Jacobus Pynacker (1672)

Another worker with the great de Keizer. He married his daughter, and at a later period helped his brother-in-law, carrying on the de Keizer tradition in red, blue, and gold. His own personal productions were signed with a monogram "J P K."

Samuel van Eenhoorn (1674)

At the sign of "The Alpha."

A member of a distinguished family of potters. He continued the traditions of the van Eenhoorns, and produced, in paleish blue, heightened with an outline in stronger colour, those charming designs, so well distributed, of flowers, foliage, birds, figures, and animals on dishes, vases, beakers, and bottles. He brought his factory to a highly flourishing state, and signed his work with a monogram of "S V E."

Gerrit Kam (1674)

At the sign of "The Three Cinder Tubs."

A good workman, with a fine conception of decorating in blue of a slightly purplish tint, notably on dishes and vases. "G K."

APPENDIX

Jan Van der Laen (1675)

He worked for a long time at the sign of "The Three Bells," both in blue and in colours, and signed with his monogram "I V L."

Lucas van Kessel (1675)

Some articles in polychrome M. Havard attributes to him. Signature "L K."

Amerensie van Kessel (1675)

Kept a shop. A few pieces in coloured ware, with a monogram, are attributed to this maker.

Arendt Cosijn (1675)

At the sign of "The Rose."

It is difficult to attribute the work turned out by a factory to any special artist, unless he has signed the produce with his initials, as well as the mark belonging to the factory. The mark of "The Rose" is well known to collectors, and little finer work was produced by any of the other factories. It produced coloured as well as blue ware, and the latter is distinguished by its charming landscapes with figures, a beautiful tone and splendid glaze. The mark was varied, consisting of the word "ROOS" or a simple "R," often surrounded with spots, while sometimes the drawing of the rose itself is the only mark.

Dirk van der Kest (1675)

At the sign of "The Boat."

He worked for many years at this factory, and his work is easily recognised by the peculiar colour of the blue, which is dark and of an inky shade; the subjects are frequently religious. He signed with his monogram in addition to the name of the factory.

Jacobus Kool (1676)

At the sign of "The Old Moor's Head."

Continued the traditions of his predecessor, J. W. Hoppestein, and signed with the initials "J K."

Simon Mes (1679)

At the sign of "The Stag."

Some early specimens with the mark of this factory are attributed to him.

M. GOUDA
1671

J. PYNACKER
1672

S. VAN EENHOORN
1674

G. P. KAM
1674

J. VAN DER LAEN
1675

L. VAN KESSEL
1675

A. VAN KESSEL
1675

A. COSIJN
1675

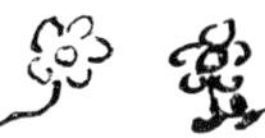

D. VAN DER KEST
1675

J. KOOL
1676

D. VAN SCHIE
1679

H. BROUWER
1679

R. J. HOPPESTEIN
1680

J. GROEN
1683

APPENDIX

Dirck van Schie (1679)

Some coarse vessels for holding milk, signed with his name in full, exist.

Huibrecht Brouwer (1679)

At the sign of "The Porcelain Axe."

He was one of the owners of this factory; but it cannot be said that all the varied pieces marked with an axe were made during his administration.

Rochus Jacobs Hoppestein (1680)

At the sign of "The Old Moor's Head."

He continued the excellent quality of his predecessors' work in blue, though not so successful in coloured ware. He signed with the initials "R I H S," as a monogram, and sometimes, but rarely, with the addition of a small design of a head.

Johannes Groen (1683)

A figure, a small statuette in coloured ware, marked with "J G" over an "R," is considered by M. Havard as probably by his hand.

Lowys Fictoor (1689)

At the sign of "The Double Jug."

A stranger, and one of the greatest potters. He has every right to be considered as having produced some of the most remarkable and beautiful work that gave to the potteries of Delft their high reputation. His finest products are splendid decorative imitations of the Chinese, both in form and colour. Those large vases and beakers, sometimes in sets of three and five, are generally ribbed or fluted, the paste is good and equal, while the surface has an oily appearance that seems only to heighten the effect of the glaze. The decoration is incomparably rich in effect of Oriental conception, consisting of foliage, flowers, birds, and insects, worked out in a scheme of red, blue, green, dark manganese, and sometimes yellow, set off by designs of scallops and borders of exquisite design and proportion.

It is singular that in this peculiar style of work there should be such a remarkable resemblance to that produced by another eminent potter, Lambertus Eenhoorn, and that both these men should have for their initials letters which, combined as monogram, so resemble each other as to be hardly distinguishable, were it not for the additional mark of the master foreman, which generally enables us to attribute a specimen to the right owner. The mark of Lowys Fictoor consists of his initials "L F" combined, sometimes with the letters "D K" or "D S K" (*Dubbelde Schenk kan,* the sign of the factory), with the addition of the initials of the foreman Jan Pietersz. A proof of the esteem he was held in is the fact that he was elected five times syndic of the Guild of St. Luke.

Adriaen Pynacker (1690)

Another great potter, and a pupil of De Keizer, whose work, though not assuming such large proportions as Lowys Fictoor's, still gave a reputation to the Delft potteries that has increased in the course of years. His decoration was quite Japanese in character, and the imitation is carried to the extreme both in fineness of quality, brilliancy of glaze, and in harmonious arrangement of blue, red and gold. The deception is complete. His models also took the fluted or channelled form, with a decoration of the brightest enamel. Besides these beautiful jugs and bottles, dishes and plates, he has also signed those charming specimens in black, with open spaces filled inwith flowers (in two teapots and two cups and saucers in the Salting collection); M. Havard has also met with some specimens in blue, which, however, add nothing to the potter's reputation. Pynacker's monogram was an "A P."

Pieter Poulisse (1690)

A stranger. Some good specimens are supposed to have come from this potter, sometimes signed with a "P." They are of striking appearance in the wealth and colour of their decoration, in which black, red and gold are the principal forces.

Theodorus Witsenbergh (1690)

At the sign of "The Star."

A stranger. He is known to have produced some fine landscape plaques, with large borders ornamented in relief, but failing his own monogram, we can only attribute those works marked with a large star to the factory he worked in.

L. FICTOOR
1689

A. PYNACKER
1690

P. POULISSE
1690

T. WITSENBERGH
1690

J. VAN DER WAL
1691

L. VAN EENHOORN
1691

P. G. KAM
1691

L. VAN DALE
1692

P. VAN DER STROOM
1693

J. DE LANGE
1694

C. VAN SCHAGEN
1694

C. VAN DER KLOOT
1695

J. VAN DER BURGEN
1695

[*face page* 90

APPENDIX

Johannes van der Wal (1691)

M. Havard awards certain specimens in blue, signed "JVDW," to this potter.

Lambertus van Eenhoorn (1691)

At the sign of "The Metal Pot."

One of the famous potters of this period. In the work he produced he may be considered as the rival of Lowys Fictoor, his contemporary. His large sets of vases have the same character, both in grandness of form and richness of decoration, as those of Fictoor, and he also produced some fine examples in blue. His monogram so resembles Fictoor's that only when countersigned by one of his foremen can the difference be noted. He had in course of time three master foremen, J. Verburg, Cornelis Kloot, and J. van der Kloot, whose initials are usually added.

Pieter G. Kam (1691)

At the sign of "The Three Cinder Tubs."

His father was the founder of this factory, and he appears to have worked there for several years, during which time the usual mark of this establishment was continued, "3 *astonne*."

Lucas van Dale (1692)

To him we owe those specimens in olive colour, with ornamented tracings in yellow, such as the small vase at the South Kensington Museum. He signed with his initials "L V D."

Pieter van der Stroom (1693)

At the sign of "The Flower Pot."

Not much is known of this master. Some of the produce of this factory has the name given—*Blompot*.

Jacobus de Lange (1694)

At the sign of "The Star."

During the years he worked, the factory retained the same quality as in the time of his predecessors; but beyond the mark of the star, there is nothing to show the master's hand. The writer had in his collection a series of plates in blue marked with the star, with the signs of the Zodiac on the border and scenes of rural and domestic life in the centre.

There are also other sets known to have come from this factory, such as the series with pictures representing whale-catching and herring fishing. The scenes are well drawn and the figures full of movement, while the colour is good and the glaze brilliant.

Cornelis van Schagen (1694)

He worked with his father at the sign of "The Claw," and certain pieces signed with his initials, "C V S," may have been by his hand.

Cornelis van der Kloot (1695)

He worked for some time as master foreman under Lambertus Eenhoorn at the sign of "The Metal Pot," and signed with his initials.

J. van der Burgen (1695)

Began as foreman to Lambertus Eenhoorn, later in the same capacity under Jacobus Pynacker at the sign of "The Porcelain Bottle," and afterwards under Kocks at "The Alpha," finishing at "The Star" under Damis

Hofdick. His signature is found on the produce of all four factories.

Cornelis Witsenburg (1696)

A stranger. M. Havard attributes a plate, with a border of flowers surrounding a coat-of-arms, and marked "C W," to this potter.

Renier Hey (1697)

At the sign of "The Roman."

Two little plaques at the Sevres Museum, representing seascapes, are signed in full with the name Reinier.

Willem Kool (1697)

At the sign of "The Three Bottles."

It is difficult to decide whether specimens in coloured ware, signed "W K," are by this potter or by Willem Kleftijus, who lived thirty years earlier.

David Kam (1697)

At the sign of "The Peacock."

The produce and its mark retain the same character as during the time of his predecessors.

P. VAN HURCH
1696

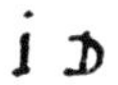

C. WITSENBURG
1696

R. HEY
1697

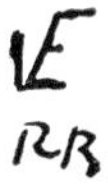

W. KOOL
1697

D. KAM
1697

J. KNOTTER
1698

VAN BROEKERHOFF
1698

Clompot.

D. BAANS
1698

I BAAN

J. DECKER
1698

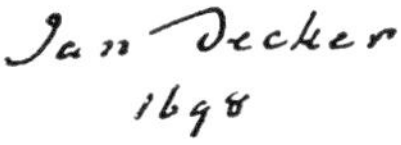

Jan Decker
1698

A. BROUWER
1699

P. S. MES
1700

VAN DER HEUL
1701

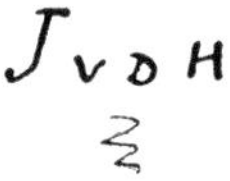

VAN SCHOONHOVEN
1702

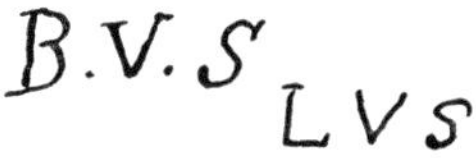

B.V.S LVS

D. HOFDICK
1705

H

[face page 94

Jan Decker (1698)

We know very little of this man. In Mr. Evenepoel's collection there are two figures, draped and crowned, signed Jan Decker with a date.

Ary Brouwer (1699)

M. Havard mentions a few pieces marked "A B," but whether by this master is uncertain.

van der Heul (1701)

At the sign of "The Alpha."

Upon the death of Pieter Kocks, shortly after he took charge of the factory, his wife had her name registered as a shopkeeper, and she sold in the shop the produce of the factory, which continued of the same kind as before. Examples marked "J V D H" are attributed to the period of her administration.

Lysbet or Bettje van Schoonhoven (1702)

At the sign of "The Claw." Bettje van Schoonhoven had her name registered as shopkeeper to this factory, and the few pieces known to be hers are said to be of fine quality. She signed with her initials "L V S" or "B V S."

Damis Hofdick (1705)

At the sign of "The Star."

M. Havard mentions several pieces signed with an "H," which he attributes to this master. Generally in blue, with open worked borders, enclosing portraits of clowns and harlequins, as well as some striking little marine scenes. Also some coloured pieces of animals, parrots, birds, etc.

Sixtius van der Sand (1705)

Not much is known of this man, still less of his work, as his mark, an involved "S," is very rare.

Joris Oosterwyk (1706)

At the sign of "The Fortune."

The marks of this pottery are as varied as its produce, consisting in the full name or initials "I H F" in different character.

APPENDIX

Willem van Dale (1707)

At the sign of "The Boat."

The produce of this factory is supposed to include some large dishes, in a dark-blue shade, decorated with subjects taken from Scripture.

Johannes Gaal (1707)

M. Havard mentions a few specimens that may be attributed to this potter, painted in colour and all of a superior kind. He signed his work with a "J G" and a cypher, and an example of his work is known bearing his name and coat-of-arms.

Mathys Boender (1713)

At the sign of "The Four Roman Heroes."

Certain specimens in blue of Oriental design, and signed "M B," are attributed to him.

Matheus van den Bogaert (1714)

He worked at three different factories, "The Flower Pot," "The Two Savages," and "The Stag." A little money-box in the Evenepoel collection, signed "M V B," is supposed to be by this master.

Abraham van Dyk (1714)

At the sign of "The Rose."

One of a number of workers at this celebrated factory, but to whom we cannot attribute directly any of the charming figure subjects in blue.

Leonard van Amsterdam (1721)

Nothing is known of this man, but there are some charming little objects, such as the backs of brushes, butter-bowls, tea-caddies in colours, in imitation of the Saxon porcelain—generally landscapes and river scenes with figures—that can be placed to his credit. The writer had amongst others a brush back, with a most elaborate border of flowers in which gold also figured, enclosing a river scene with a man fishing. These specimens are sometimes signed "V A" or "A V;" but even without the mark they are quite recognisable.

Cornelis de Berg (1730)

At the sign of "The Star."

During his occupancy of this factory, its work reached a high state of development,

S. VAN DER SAND
1705

J. OOSTERWYCK
1706

J : H : F
3 0 7
in't fortuyn

J. H. T
in't fortuyn

J. GAAL
1707

IG
34

M. BOENDER
1713

MB

M. VAN DEN BOGAERT
1714

MVB
1757

L. VAN AMSTERDAM
1721

VA V AV

C. DE BERG
1720

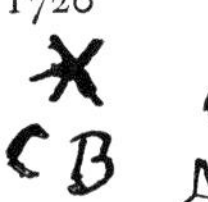

P. VAN DER STROOM
1725

P VDS.

F. VAN HESSE
1730

J-C S
R

J-C. S
R

Z. DEXTRA
1720

Z. DEX.

H. & G. DE KONING
1721

G d K H D K

P. VIZEER
1752

P Vizeer

and the beautiful specimens in blue are of the finest Delft produce, not only in imitation of Oriental china, but also showing a marked personality of the artist's decorative talents. The marks are numerous and varied. Among this factory's workers at this period was Aalmis, whose work is described under the heading Rotterdam.

Frederic van Hesse (1730)

His name in full occurring on a coloured plaque and a large number of various specimens with his initials, accompanied by the letter "R," lead us to suppose that he was one of the numerous workers at that celebrated and successful factory "The Rose."

Hendrick Zieremans (1757)

This man's signature in full on a small coloured jug is all we know about his work.

Zacharias Dextra (1720)

At the sign of "The Three Tuns."

One of two of this name who produced some fine examples in coloured ware, his signature being "Z. DEX."

Hendrik and Gilles de Koning (1721)

At the sign of the Double Jug.

Judging from the initials, both seem to have worked in the Oriental style with those rich combinations of blue, red, and gold. The writer had in his collection two cups and saucers signed with the marks of these men, very similar in character to the work of Adriaen Pynacker and A. Reygensbergh.

Piet Vizeer (1752)

What we know of this potter's work is rather varied in character. There is a coloured plaque, signed with his name in full, representing a cock, described by Mr. Demmin in his collection as being one of the marvels of Delft pottery, but then Mr. Demmin's geese are mostly swans. Another is cited by M. Havard, belonging to the Loudon collection, two coloured plaques representing the arms of Orange. Finally, we have two square blue plaques of Scriptural subjects in the British Museum, but the writer has not been able to verify the signature. At all events, this artist has obtained a mysterious reputation that he is hardly entitled to.

APPENDIX

Justus de Berg (1759)

At the sign of "The Star."

His initials, accompanied with a star, show that his work was in every way in keeping with the reputation of this factory.

Anthoni Kruisweg (1759)

At the sign of "The Old Moor's Head."

The two gourd-shaped bottles in blue at the Victoria and Albert Museum, representing marine plants and insects, and the similar two of the same size and shape, with decoration of tulips, peonies, and other flowers, belonging to Mr. Salting, at the same museum, are excellent specimens of this artist's graceful and decorative work. The two latter specimens belonged at one time to the writer. They are signed with the maker's monogram.

Johannes Pennis (1759)

At the sign of "The Porcelain Dish."

This artist is known for his curious plates, inscribed with verses and lines of music, and he signed with a varied form of "P."

Kornelis van Dyck (1759)

At the sign of "The Claw."

A few pieces marked with these initials and the claw are attributed to this potter.

Willem van der Does (1764)

At the sign of "The Three Bells."

He carried on this factory, but nothing special is to be noted as coming from his hand.

Pieter van Doorne (1759)

At the sign of "The Porcelain Bottle."

His monogram of "P V D" does not distinguish his work from that of his predecessors.

Johannes Verhagen (1759)

At the sign of "The New Moor's Head."

Verhagen considerably influenced the artistic trend of pottery, and raised it more to the level it had acquired a century before. He sometimes borrowed his figure subjects from the prints of Goltius, and even in his successful ventures he managed to surround his subjects with beautifully executed borders,

J. DE BERG
1759

* *
JB J:B

A. KRUISWEG
1759

AK

J. PENNIS
1759

P P

K. VAN DYCK
1759

K VD

W. VAN DER DOES
1764

WD

P. VAN DOORNE
1759

PD

P. PAREE
1759

NP NP

J. VERHAGEN
1759

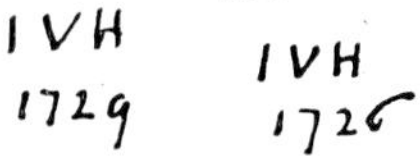

IVH IVH
1729 1726

P. VAN DER BURGH
1759

PB B·P
Clompot

A. PENNIS
1759

AP

J. T. DEXTRA
1759

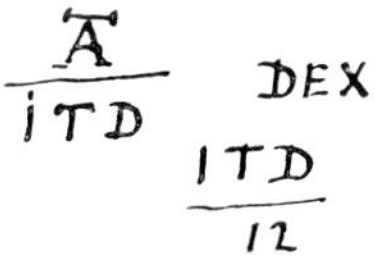

A
ITD DEX
ITD
12

P. VAN MARUM
1759

M PVM

DE MILDE
1759

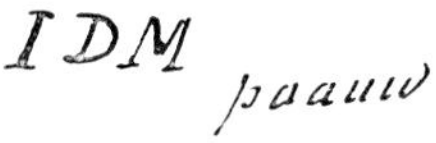

IDM paauw

showing a grace and arrangement of floral design that placed his work far beyond that of most of his contemporaries. His initials, "I V H" with a date, are frequently met with.

Paulus van der Bergh (1759)

At the sign of "The Flower Pot."

A monogram of the letters "P V B," together with the name of the factory, is about all we know of this potter's work.

Pieter Paree (1759)

At the sign of "The Metal Pot."

Specimens with this factory's mark are supposed to have been turned out during this master's period.

Anthony Pennis (1759)

At the sign of "The Two Little Boats."

Several examples in coloured ware, such as butter-bowls in the shape of vegetables, cabbages, artichokes, etc., in blue and green, signed with his monogram, may be considered as coming from this master.

JAN THEUNIS DEXTRA (1759)

At the sign of "The Alpha."

A number of articles signed with "I T D" or a simple "D" or "D E X" show the kind of varied work produced by this potter; they are, however, rarely accompanied by the initial of the factory, "A."

PETRUS VAN MARUM (1759)

At the sign of "The Roman."

His work is not particularly interesting though of considerable variety, generally in blue, with ornaments and coats of arms. He signed his work with a varied monogram or his initials, "P V M."

JACOBUS DE MILDE (1759)

At the sign of "The Peacock."

He signed with his initials as well as the mark of the factory while he worked there.

DIRCK VAN DER DOES (1759)

At the sign of "The Rose."

He signed with his initials "D V D D," and M. Havard has met with some specimens marked with a rose, but these are rare.

APPENDIX

Gerrit Brouwer (1759)

At the sign of "The Jug."

The work of this factory is not particularly remarkable for its quality, and the mark "L P K" varies considerably in the form and writing of the letters.

Justus Brouwer (1759)

At the sign of "The Porcelain Axe."

The mark of this factory is well known, and although coloured ware was produced, it is better known for its blue work. The series of plates representing whale-catching and herring-fishing are in drawing, colour, and glaze of high quality and good workmanship. Some specimens marked with an "I B" are attributed to Brouwer.

Pieter van den Briel (1759)

At the sign of "The Fortune."

His widow carried on the business after his death, and signed with the letters "W V D B"—Widow van den Briel.

Johannes den Appel (1759)

At the sign of "The Boat."

Not much is known of this potter. M. Havard cites a small coloured model of a cow, signed, but the mark does not necessarily attribute the cow to den Appel, and the letter "A" bears a curious resemblance to the sign of "The Alpha."

Hendrick van Hoorn (1759)

At the sign of "The Three Cinder Tubs."

His coloured work, in which often the blue and green predominate, is rather rich in appearance, and his initials are sometimes met with on butter-bowls, taking the shape of fruit and vegetables, baskets, and such like, but he also worked in blue. A specimen, according to M. Havard, is in the Evenepoel collection with his full signature.

Gysbert Verhaast (1760)

A great man in his day, though we do not know much about him. The few pieces he has left show us a most skilled draughtsman decorating some fine plaques, both with landscapes and interiors, with figures in colours, and signed with his signature in full.

D. VAN DER DOES
1759

DVDD DvD

D

G. BROUWER
1759

LPKan
lpk

J. BROUWER
1759

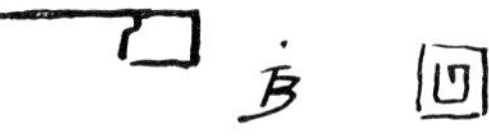

VAN DEN BRIEL
1759

PvDB
WvDB

J. DEN APPEL
1759

IDA IDA

H. VAN HOORN
1759

HvH 3
astonne

G. VERHAAST
1760

G Verhaast.

T. SPAANDONCK
1764

DSK DSK

G. VERSTELLE
1764

G:V:S
GVS
S.VS 4

H. VAN MIDDELDYK
1764

HVMD
1754 MDK

W. VAN BEEK
1764

W:V:B

APPENDIX

Thomas Spaandonck (1764)

At the sign of "The Double Jug."

We have only the initials of the factory, "D S K" (*Dubbelde Schenk Kan*), to go by; but the specimens available clearly show the degenerating work of this period, and they may have been made during this potter's control of the factory.

Geertruy Verstelle (1764)

At the sign of "The Old Moor's Head."

A number of specimens, with the initials "G V S," in various forms are met with; but they all bear testimony to the declining state of this once celebrated pottery.

Hendrick van Middeldyk (1764)

At the sign of "The Stag."

The mark of this potter frequently occurs in various forms, often with the addition of a date; but there is nothing of importance in the work he did, either in blue or in colour.

Willem van Beek (1764)

At the sign of "The Two Savages."

Little is known of this potter's work, and

what we have, signed with his initials, "W V B," is of a very ordinary kind.

Hugo Brouwer (1764)

At the sign of "The Three Porcelain Bottles."

A number of specimens are met with bearing the initials of this potter. An interesting plaque, showing the encroaching of the sea at Scheveningen during a storm, is in the possession of the Queen of Holland.

Albertus Kiell (1764)

At the sign of "The Star."

During this potter's tenure of the celebrated Star the work continued to deteriorate. His signature, "A K" with a star, is frequently met with.

Johannes van Duyn (1764)

At the sign of "The Porcelain Dish."

His signature, V. Duyn, in full, is often met with, both on blue and coloured specimens of great variety in quality; but some of the little jugs and figures are quite charming.

H. BROUWER
1764

HB H B

A. KIELL
1764

A : K : AK

J. VAN DUYN
1764

I Duijn
Duijn

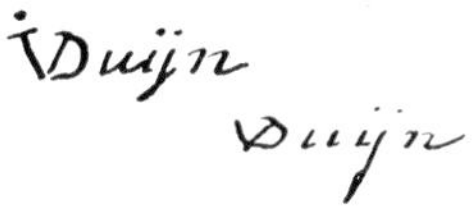

L. SANDERUS
1764

J. VAN DER KLOOT
1764

I V K

J. HALDER
1765

A
I : H

A
I H

J. HARLEES
1770

HL HL

A. VAN DER KEEL
1780

l pet kan

D. HARLEES
1795

D H

J. VAN PUTTEN & CO.
1830

I V P & C

J. AALMIS

I Aalmis

IAalmis
Rotterdam

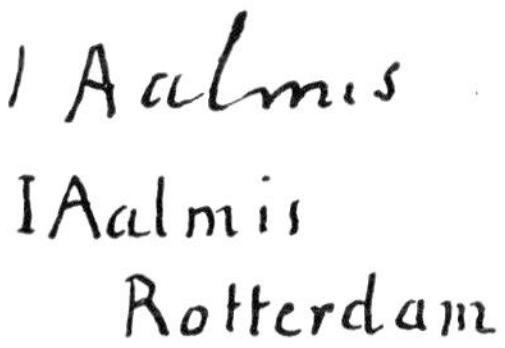

AMSTERDAM

APPENDIX

Lambertus Sanderus (1764)

At the sign of "The Claw."

He no doubt signed the produce of this factory during the time of his occupation of it.

Johannes van der Kloot (1764)

At the sign of "The Roman."

We are not sure whether certain specimens marked "I V K" can be attributed to this potter.

Jacobus Halder (1765)

At the sign of "The Alpha."

His signature with the mark of the factory frequently occurs on figures and animals, often of a small size.

Johannes Harlees (1770)

At the sign of "The Porcelain Bottle."

Sets of vases and beakers in blue are signed with the initials of this potter and the mark of the bottle.

Hendrick Janszoon (1779)

At the sign of "The Rose."

M. Havard mentions that at this period

"The Rose" became a tile factory. So the glory of this once celebrated factory passed away.

Arend de Haak (1780)

The same distinguished writer cites this potter as the first to imitate the English ware of Turner.

Abraham van der Keel (1780)

At the sign of "The Jug."

His signature, written in full with the date 1791, occurs on a jug, in blue, of a common order.

Dirk Harlees (1795)

At the sign of "The Porcelain Bottle."

His initials, "D H L," and the mark of the factory, occur on blue plates.

Piccardt (1800)

At the sign of "The Porcelain Bottle."

An Englishman, a soldier, took up this factory. It now became a kiln for fireproof bricks.

WEESP

AMSTERDAM

Amstel

Amstel

LOOSDREGHT

Möl

* Mòl

THE HAGUE
S'GRAVENHAGE
S'HAGE

[*face page* 110

APPENDIX

Sanderson and Bellaert (1808)

These potters were responsible for further introducing the English ware of Turner. Sanderson was an Englishman.

J. van Putten & Co. (1830)

M. Havard mentions this firm as being formed out of the remains of "The Three Bells," "The Claw," and "The Rose." It is the last song of the swan, and some of the work turned out will bear favourable comparison with the ware produced in olden days.

INDEX

*** References are indicated in the following manner :—

To Potter's marks, by *large roman* numerals indicating the number of the plate on which they occur. These plates of Potters' marks are to be found between pages 74 and 110.

To Preliminary matter and *Illustration plates*, by *small roman* numerals.

To the Text, by numerals in ordinary type, thus—

Verstelle, Geertruy, IX ; *Illustration plate*, xlviii ; 107.
Havard, Henri, *prelim.* xii ; 36, 37, etc.

INDEX

INDEX

INDEX

INDEX

THE END

PRINTED BY
WILLIAM CLOWES AND SONS, LIMITED,
LONDON AND BECCLES.